Budgeting Without a Spreadsheet

A Simple System for People Who Won't Track Every Dollar

Willa Crenshaw

First edition, 2026

Published by Willa Crenshaw

Contents

Chapter 1: The Spreadsheet Struggle is Real

The chipped Formica countertop felt cool under my forearm as I stared at the screen. Not a spreadsheet *on* the counter, mind you – that would be ridiculous. This was a spreadsheet *of* spreadsheets. A meta-spreadsheet, if you will.

That feeling – that low-humming dread of opening the budget file – is far more common than anyone admits. We tell ourselves we need to be diligent, meticulous. That financial control demands constant vigilance. But what if the very tools designed to *give* us control are actually sabotaging our efforts? What if the problem isn't a lack of willpower or discipline, but an overabundance of...well, everything? Complexity is a tax on your attention, and in today's world, your attention is the scarcest resource you have.

I know what you're thinking: "But surely, detailed tracking is important! How can you improve if you don't know where every dollar goes?" It's a valid point. And it's also precisely the trap most of us fall into. We get so focused on *measuring* our finances that we forget to actually *live* them. It's like obsessively monitoring your running pace while forgetting to enjoy the scenery, or meticulously photographing every dish you cook instead of actually tasting the food. The process becomes more important than the purpose.

Consider Mark Cuban. Not the billionaire investor, though his experience is relevant. I'm talking about Mark Cuban, plumber, from Dayton, Ohio. He called my radio show a few years back, exasperated. He wasn't looking for investment advice; he was looking for help with budgeting. "I work hard," he said, voice thick with frustration, "but every month it's the same story. I know *something* is off, but by the time I get home from a 12-hour shift, the last thing I want to do is sit down and figure out where all the money went." He'd downloaded several apps, tried online templates, even attempted a handwritten ledger. Nothing stuck. It wasn't that he was bad with money; it was that his life didn't neatly fit into pre-defined categories and formulas. He needed simplicity, not sophistication.

Mark isn't an outlier. In fact, he represents the vast majority of people: the seventy percent who consistently struggle with traditional budgeting methods. Another twenty percent can make it work – but only with a lot of effort, a constant internal negotiation between wanting to feel in control and feeling overwhelmed by the process. That leaves just ten percent for whom detailed tracking is genuinely enjoyable, almost therapeutic. They thrive on data. They *like* seeing everything laid out in neat rows and columns. And that's fantastic…for them. But trying to force the other ninety percent into that mold is a recipe for failure.

They aren't lazy or irresponsible. They simply have different priorities, different brain wiring. Maybe they're big-picture oriented, focused on long-term goals rather than daily details. Or maybe they just have a lot on their plate – demanding jobs, families to raise, lives to live – and can't devote hours each week to managing every penny. Forcing yourself into a spreadsheet-centric system is usually counterproductive. It adds stress, diminishes motivation, and ultimately leads to abandonment. You end up feeling worse about your finances than when you started.

Think of it like learning a new language. You can memorize grammar rules and vocabulary lists until the cows come home, but if you never actually *speak* the language, you'll never become fluent. Budgeting is the same. It's not about mastering complex techniques; it's about developing healthy habits that align with your lifestyle. And those habits need to be sustainable – something you can maintain week after week, month after month, without feeling like you're running a marathon.

I remember speaking with a woman named Eleanor, a kindergarten teacher in Atlanta. She described her budgeting attempts as "a constant cycle of hope and despair." She'd start strong each January, meticulously tracking every expense, but by February she'd be completely derailed. "It felt like I was punishing myself," she confessed. "I'm already exhausted from dealing with 25 five-year-olds all day. Coming home to a spreadsheet just felt... oppressive." Eleanor wasn't lacking financial knowledge; she lacked a system that accommodated her energy levels and priorities. She needed something gentle, forgiving, and – crucially – easy to maintain.

The cost of inaction isn't simply missed savings opportunities or accumulating debt. It's the erosion of your peace of mind. The constant anxiety about money. The feeling of being trapped in a cycle of financial insecurity. It's missing out on experiences you enjoy because you're afraid to spend. It's sacrificing long-term goals for short-term comfort. That weight, that subtle but persistent drain on your emotional energy, is far more damaging than any single missed budget category.

You might be wondering: if detailed tracking doesn't work for most people, what *does*? The answer, surprisingly, lies in simplicity. In focusing not on meticulous measurement, but on strategic allocation. In understanding that you don't need to know exactly where every dollar goes, just that your money is working for *you*.

We're going to talk about a system I call "The Three Envelope Rule." It's based on the idea of dividing your income into three broad categories: Essentials, Savings, and Freedom. It's an adaptation of the traditional envelope budgeting method – physically separating cash into labeled envelopes – but streamlined for the digital age. We won't be dealing with actual paper envelopes (unless you really want to!), but rather with a mental framework for prioritizing your spending.

The beauty of this system is its flexibility. You can adjust the percentages based on your individual circumstances and priorities. You're not locked into rigid categories or forced to conform to someone else's idea of what "responsible" budgeting looks like. It's about creating a system that works *for* you, not against you.

This isn't about deprivation. It's about empowerment. About recognizing that you have choices and making those choices consciously, instead of reactively. It's about shifting your focus from restriction to intention. From guilt to gratitude. From spreadsheets and formulas to a life lived with financial peace of mind.

Imagine this: You open your bank account at the end of the month, not with dread, but with curiosity. Not to pore over every transaction, but to check that your core priorities are being met. You see that your Essentials are covered, your Savings are on track, and you have a comfortable amount left for whatever brings you joy. That feeling – that sense of calm confidence – is worth far more than any meticulously balanced spreadsheet.

The next step isn't downloading another app or creating another template. It's something far simpler: picking up a pen and paper, closing your eyes for a moment, and asking yourself one question. What truly matters to you? Because the most effective budget isn't about controlling your spending; it's about aligning your money with your values. And that starts with clarity—knowing exactly what those values *are*.

...that feeling – that sense of calm confidence – is worth far more than any meticulously balanced spreadsheet. The next step isn't downloading another app or creating another template. It's something far simpler: picking up a pen and paper, closing your eyes for a moment, and asking yourself one question. What truly matters to you? Because the most effective budget isn't about controlling your spending; it's about aligning your money with your values. And that starts with clarity—knowing exactly what those values *are*.

I remember back in 2019, convinced I was on the verge of financial enlightenment. Sunday afternoon, coffee brewing, screen glowing... I spent an entire day building what I thought was the perfect budget spreadsheet – forty-seven categories, color-coded tabs for everything from 'artisanal dog treats' to 'unexpected plumbing,' formulas that would auto-calculate everything down to the penny. The thing looked like a NASA control panel. I felt like a financial genius. Three weeks later? I realized I'd updated it exactly once and had completely lost track of my actual spending. The system was so complex, so demanding of attention, I'd rather ignore my finances than face it. It wasn't laziness; it was sheer overwhelm. A beautifully crafted cage is still a cage.

The frustration isn't unique to me, or even to the spreadsheet-averse. It's built into the very premise of most financial advice: that control comes from *more* data, *more* categorization, *more* tracking. That if you just had a better system for documenting every single transaction, you'd magically solve your money problems. But what if the problem isn't a lack of information? What if it's a lack of connection to what truly matters?

Take Mark, a lawyer I consulted with last year. He was an analytical guy—loved data, thrived on optimization—and genuinely enjoyed building spreadsheets. He had one that was legendary among his friends: meticulously detailed, flawlessly accurate, and… utterly paralyzing. "I spend so much time *maintaining* the thing," he confessed, "that I actually avoid looking at it. It feels like a constant audit of my life, a judgment on every single purchase." The spreadsheet hadn't liberated him; it had imprisoned him in a cycle of guilt and anxiety. He knew where his money was going, but he felt worse about it than ever before.

Mark's story illustrates the core fallacy: detailed tracking isn't inherently valuable. It's only valuable if it leads to meaningful action—to choices that align with your values. If you're simply recording data without reflecting on what it means, you're just creating a more elaborate form of denial. It's like meticulously documenting every ingredient in a cake while simultaneously ignoring the fact that you hate cake.

The truth is, most of us aren't wired to enjoy granular tracking. Our brains are designed for pattern recognition and big-picture thinking, not for obsessively categorizing expenses. We're storytellers, meaning-makers, not accountants. And when we try to force ourselves into a system that doesn't align with our natural tendencies, we inevitably rebel.

Think about the last time you tried to adopt a new habit – learning an instrument, starting a fitness routine, mastering a new skill. What happened if you made it overly complicated? If you set unrealistic expectations and demanded perfection from day one? You probably gave up. It's the same with budgeting. The more complex and demanding the system, the less likely you are to stick with it.

It's not about being "bad with money," either. I've worked with doctors, engineers, CEOs – people who are brilliant in their respective fields—and consistently see them struggle with the same basic budgeting pitfalls. The issue isn't intelligence or capability; it's that traditional financial advice often ignores the fundamental principles of human psychology. It assumes we're rational actors motivated by self-interest, when in reality we're emotional creatures driven by values and priorities.

Consider Emily, a high school teacher with two young children. She desperately wanted to save for her kids' college education but felt constantly overwhelmed by financial obligations. Every month was a scramble to make ends meet. She'd tried several budgeting apps, each promising to simplify the process, but they all left her feeling more stressed than before.

"It wasn't about not having enough money," she explained. "It was about not knowing *where* it was going and feeling like I had no control. Every time I opened the app, I just felt defeated." Emily wasn't lacking discipline; she was lacking a system that acknowledged the realities of her life: unpredictable expenses, long work hours, and the constant demands of raising a family. She needed something simple, flexible, and forgiving—something that wouldn't punish her for occasional slip-ups.

Emily's story isn't an outlier. It represents a pattern I've observed time and time again: people don't fail at budgeting because they lack willpower; they fail because they use systems that are fundamentally incompatible with their lives. They get bogged down in the details, lose sight of the bigger picture, and ultimately abandon the process altogether.

The alternative isn't to throw your hands up in despair and resign yourself to financial chaos. It's to embrace a different approach—one that prioritizes clarity over precision, alignment over control, and values over spreadsheets.

Imagine this: You wake up on a Saturday morning, not dreading the task of budgeting, but feeling excited about taking control of your finances. Not by meticulously tracking every expense, but by consciously aligning your spending with what truly matters to you. You know exactly where your money is going because you've already made those decisions in advance. You feel confident and empowered, knowing that you're building a future that reflects your values and priorities.

That feeling—that sense of calm confidence—is within reach. It doesn't require hours of spreadsheet work or complicated financial calculations. It simply requires a shift in perspective: from controlling every penny to prioritizing what truly matters. From obsessing over the details to focusing on the big picture. And that starts with asking yourself one simple question: What truly matters to you?

Because when your money reflects your values, budgeting isn't a chore; it's an act of self-respect. It's a way of saying, "My life is worth investing in." And that's a powerful realization.

But let's be real for a second. I know what some of you are thinking: "This sounds good in theory, but what about the practicalities? How do you actually make this work?" You might be picturing yourself abandoning all tracking and simply hoping for the best. Or perhaps you're worried that without detailed data, you'll lose control and fall back into old habits.

Those are valid concerns. And it's true that blindly ignoring your finances isn't a solution. The key is to find a middle ground—a system that provides enough clarity and accountability without becoming overly burdensome. It's about creating a framework that supports your values and allows you to make conscious choices, not one that dictates every aspect of your financial life.

We will be moving away from the idea of 'restriction' when it comes to money – the feeling that budgeting requires deprivation or sacrifice. Instead, we'll focus on *intentionality*. Giving every dollar a job isn't about limiting what you can enjoy; it's about maximizing the impact of your spending and ensuring that you're getting the most value out of every purchase. It's about consciously choosing where your money goes so that it aligns with your values and goals, not simply reacting to impulses or societal expectations.

Think of a sculptor crafting a masterpiece. They don't randomly chip away at the stone; they have a clear vision in mind and carefully remove everything that doesn't contribute to that vision. Your money is like that stone: you can sculpt it into something beautiful and meaningful, but only if you start with a clear understanding of what you want to create.

We're going to explore a system built on simplicity, automation, and a focus on aligning your spending with your core priorities. It doesn't rely on obsessively tracking every transaction; instead, it focuses on establishing clear spending limits in key areas and then letting the system do the work for you. Think of it less like accounting and more like setting guardrails—providing structure without stifling creativity or enjoyment.

And to be blunt, this isn't a magical fix-all. It won't instantly solve all your financial problems. But it *will* give you a solid foundation for building better habits, reducing stress, and taking control of your finances – even if the very word "spreadsheet" makes you break out in hives. The journey toward financial well-being isn't about perfection; it's about progress. It's about making small, sustainable changes that add up over time. And it starts with a single question: What truly matters to you? Consider that question for the next 24 hours before we dig into how to translate those values into concrete action.

...guardrails—providing structure without stifling creativity or enjoyment. And to be blunt, this isn't a magical fix-all. It won't instantly solve all your financial problems. But it *will* give you a solid foundation for building better habits, reducing stress, and taking control of your finances – even if the very word "spreadsheet" makes you break out in hives. The journey toward financial well-being isn't about perfection; it's about progress. It's about making small, sustainable changes that add up over time. And it starts with a single question: What truly matters to you? Consider that question for the next 24 hours before we dig into how to translate those values into concrete action.

Let's be honest, though. That 'considering' part? It feels...soft. Like another one of those self-help exercises where you're supposed to journal and meditate your way to a better life. And I get it. You might be thinking: "Okay, this sounds good in theory, but what about the actual numbers? What if I have no idea what my priorities even *are* when it comes to money?" Or maybe you're picturing yourself staring into the abyss of your bank statements, completely lost and overwhelmed.

You're not wrong to feel that way. It's easy to get paralyzed by the sheer weight of financial uncertainty. But here's a secret: clarifying your values isn't about achieving some enlightened state of mind overnight. It's about starting small—with one or two things that genuinely bring you joy, and then building from there.

I remember back in 2019, completely convinced I was cracking the code to financial freedom with my elaborate spreadsheet. Forty-seven categories, color-coded tabs...it was a masterpiece of organization. I felt like a financial genius. Three weeks later, though?

It sat untouched. The system was so complex, so demanding of my attention, that I'd rather ignore my finances altogether than face it. That Sunday afternoon, meticulously inputting every expense, felt less like taking control and more like building an elaborate prison for myself.

The truth is, our brains aren't wired for endless data entry. We crave simplicity. We thrive on momentum. And when a system feels burdensome—when the effort required outweighs the perceived benefit—we naturally resist it. It's not about willpower; it's about neurobiology. Your attention is a finite resource and constantly being pulled in a dozen directions. Demanding hours of detailed tracking each week? That's asking for failure.

Think about Maria, a librarian I consulted with last year. She loved her job—surrounded by books, helping people discover new worlds—but she was drowning in student loan debt. She'd tried every budgeting app under the sun, but nothing stuck. They all felt too…clinical. Too focused on restriction.

"It just made me feel guilty," she confessed. "Like I was punishing myself for enjoying life." She'd meticulously log a $5 latte, then berate herself for not brewing coffee at home. The joy of that small indulgence was completely overshadowed by the weight of financial judgment. She wasn't trying to be irresponsible; she simply wanted to live a full and meaningful life without sacrificing her happiness.

Maria's story is so common because it gets to the heart of why traditional budgeting often fails: It treats money as an enemy, something to be controlled and suppressed, rather than as a tool to enable a better life. We're told to cut back, sacrifice, and deprive ourselves in the name of financial responsibility. But that approach rarely works long-term because it ignores our fundamental human need for pleasure and enjoyment.

What if, instead, we reframed budgeting as an act of self-care? As a way to consciously allocate resources towards the things that truly matter—the experiences, relationships, and values that give our lives meaning? What if we focused on *funding* our priorities rather than simply restricting our spending?

That shift in perspective can be transformative. It changes budgeting from a chore into an opportunity. From a source of stress into a source of empowerment. And it starts with asking yourself: "What kind of life do I actually want to live?" Not what society tells you you *should* want, but what genuinely brings you joy and fulfillment?

Maybe it's traveling the world. Maybe it's spending more time with family and friends. Maybe it's pursuing a passion project or making a difference in your community. Whatever it is, those are the things worth prioritizing—the things that deserve to be funded first. Not after all the "essential" expenses are covered, but as an integral part of your financial plan.

Consider the example of Ben, a software engineer I worked with recently. He was obsessed with minimalism and had meticulously optimized his life to minimize spending. He drove a beat-up car, lived in a tiny apartment, and rarely went out for entertainment. He'd saved a considerable amount of money, but he wasn't happy.

"I feel like I'm just existing," he told me. "I have all this money, but I don't know what to do with it. I've sacrificed everything that brings me joy in the name of financial security." He realized he'd become so focused on saving for a distant future that he'd forgotten to actually *live* in the present moment. He hadn't booked a vacation or taken a class in years and rarely saw his friends.

Ben's story is a cautionary tale—a reminder that financial well-being isn't just about accumulating wealth; it's about creating a life that aligns with your values and brings you joy. It's about finding the sweet spot between security and fulfillment. And sometimes, that means spending money on things that are purely enjoyable—even if they don't fit neatly into a budget category.

Because here's the thing: Life is unpredictable. Things will inevitably go wrong. Unexpected expenses will arise. And when those moments happen, having a little bit of breathing room in your budget can make all the difference. It can prevent you from going into debt or derailing your long-term goals.

That's why we're not aiming for perfect restriction; we're aiming for intentional allocation. We want to create a system that allows you to spend money on the things you love without feeling guilty or stressed. A system that supports your values and enables you to live a life that is both financially secure *and* personally fulfilling.

So, before you start mapping out your budget, take a few moments to reflect on what truly matters to you. What are your priorities? What brings you joy? And how can you consciously allocate your resources towards those things? Don't overthink it. Start with one or two simple goals and build from there. Remember, this isn't about deprivation; it's about empowerment. It's about creating a financial life that is aligned with your values and supports the life you want to live.

Now, close your eyes for just a moment. Picture yourself six months from now, feeling confident and in control of your finances. You're not stressed about money; you're enjoying your life. You're able to pursue your passions, spend time with loved ones, and save for the future—all without sacrificing your happiness. What does that feel like? Hold onto that image. Because that's what we're working towards. And it all starts with a single question: Where will you direct *your* money tomorrow?

I gave up on the meta-spreadsheet around 11 PM that Sunday. Not because I couldn't make it work—I absolutely could have. That was the problem.

The cold metal felt strangely comforting. It was a reminder that sometimes, control isn't about mastering every detail, but about choosing *what* to focus on.

Chapter 2: Understanding Your Cash Flow

When was the last time you could name—without checking your phone—how much money is in your checking account right now? Not the rough range. The actual number.

I was sitting in a Starbucks on Clark Street in Chicago when I first understood how broken this whole thing is. Tuesday morning, maybe seven-thirty. The line stretched almost to the door. Everyone doing the same choreography: grab phone, check work email while shuffling forward, order without looking up, tap to pay, grab drink, leave.

Two women ahead of me, mid-thirties probably, both in those expensive-looking workout clothes that somehow signal "I have a Peloton at home." One of them pulled out her phone to pay and just... stopped. Stared at the screen. Her friend noticed.

"You good?"

"I just—" The woman shook her head, this tiny bewildered gesture. "I have no idea where my money went this month."

Not panicked. Not angry. Bewildered. Like she'd misplaced her keys except the keys were several thousand dollars and she genuinely could not remember the last time she'd seen them.

Her friend laughed—that knowing, sympathetic laugh that says *oh honey, same*—and said, "Every month. Every single month."

The barista was waiting. The woman paid. They grabbed their drinks and left.

I've thought about that moment at least once a week for five years now. Because it captures something most personal finance books completely miss, something I didn't even understand myself until I'd spent hundreds of hours sitting across from people trying to figure out where their money went: the blank confusion that settles over you when you earn a reasonable income, you're not buying yachts or booking weekly spa days, you're just *living*—just getting coffee and paying rent and buying groceries and existing in the world—and somehow, at the end of the month, there's almost nothing left.

You look at your account balance and you genuinely cannot reconstruct where it went. The money just evaporated. Vanished like steam.

That feeling—that specific cocktail of confusion and low-grade dread—is what happens when you don't have a clear picture of your cash flow. And here's what nobody tells you, what the spreadsheet people and the app developers and the financial advisors all skip right over: it's not about irresponsibility. It's not about lack of discipline.

It's about invisibility.

Most of your money leaves your life so quietly, so automatically, so seamlessly woven into the background hum of modern existence, that tracking it feels like trying to count oxygen molecules in the air. You know it's happening. You just can't see it.

But here's the cost of not knowing. And I mean the real cost, the human cost, not the abstract financial-advisor version where someone in a suit tells you you're losing compound interest or failing to maximize your retirement contributions or whatever other bloodless abstraction they're selling.

Jennifer worked as a nurse practitioner at Northwestern Memorial. Eighty-seven thousand a year. Solid income, especially for someone without kids, without a mortgage, without the obvious big expenses everyone talks about. She drove a five-year-old Honda Civic she'd bought used from a CarMax in the suburbs. Lived in a decent one-bedroom in Ravenswood—not trendy but not dangerous, the kind of neighborhood where the coffee shops aren't trying too hard. She didn't collect anything, didn't have expensive hobbies, didn't travel much beyond maybe one trip a year to see her sister in Portland.

And every single month, she felt broke.

Not actually broke—her rent cleared, her lights stayed on, she wasn't missing meals—but that creeping, background-radiation sensation that she was always one unexpected expense away from real trouble. The feeling that the ground beneath her was thinner than it should be. Like she was walking on ice that looked solid but might not be.

She'd lie awake on Sunday nights doing mental arithmetic. Eyes open in the dark, ceiling fan going, running calculations in her head: "Okay, if I need new tires next month—and I probably do, that back left one's been looking worn since March—I can push off that dentist appointment. The filling's not hurting yet. It can wait. Or maybe I can pick up an extra overnight shift. Two, if they're available. That's another six hundred before taxes, maybe four-fifty after, minus the extra I'll spend on takeout because there's no way I'm cooking after a twelve-hour overnight..."

This is a woman earning nearly six figures. Playing financial Jenga in her head at eleven PM on a work night, trying to figure out how to afford a basic car repair.

The breaking point came in April. Her best friend from college—they'd been roommates sophomore and junior year, stayed close after graduation even as life pulled them to different cities—called to say she was getting married. Asked Jennifer to be maid of honor.

And Jennifer's first emotion—before joy, before excitement, before any of the things you're supposed to feel when someone you love is happy—was panic.

Pure, stomach-dropping panic.

Because she knew exactly what was coming. The dress, which would be whatever the bride picked and probably two hundred dollars, maybe more if the bride had expensive taste. The shoes that match the dress. The bachelorette weekend—probably Nashville or Miami or Austin, somewhere you fly to, somewhere with hotels and restaurants and activities that cost money. The bridal shower gift. The wedding gift. The hair and makeup for the actual day because you can't show up in the photos looking like you did your own hair in a Holiday Inn bathroom. Easily two thousand dollars. Probably closer to three if she was being honest.

And she had no idea where she'd get it.

She actually considered saying no. To her best friend. To someone she'd known since freshman year, someone who'd held her hair back when she was sick sophomore year, someone who'd driven four hours from Milwaukee when Jennifer's mom died. She almost said no because she couldn't figure out how to find two thousand dollars despite earning eighty-seven thousand dollars a year.

Think about that. Sit with it for a second. A woman making nearly ninety grand, seriously contemplating whether she could afford to be in her best friend's wedding.

She said yes, obviously. You don't say no to that. But she felt sick about it for weeks. Woke up anxious, that specific 4 AM anxiety where your brain just starts running scenarios and won't stop. Checked her bank balance compulsively, like the number might be different than it was ten minutes ago, like maybe money would just appear if she refreshed enough times.

That's what "not understanding your cash flow" actually costs you.

It's not numbers on a screen. It's not abstract. It's lying awake doing math when you should be sleeping. It's the stomach-drop when someone asks you to do something that should be joyful. It's the constant background hum of financial anxiety that follows you everywhere, colors every decision, turns every invitation into a calculation, makes you feel broke when objectively you aren't. Makes you feel like you're failing at something everyone else seems to have figured out.

I've seen this play out dozens of times now, and the pattern is always the same: capable people, earning decent money, living reasonably, who nonetheless feel like they're treading water. Who can't say yes to things they want to say yes to. Who carry this low-grade financial anxiety like background music they can't turn off.

And here's what gets me—what still gets me, even after all these years doing this work—it's always framed as a personal failing. Like if you just had more discipline, more willpower, more whatever, you'd have this figured out. But I'm going to tell you something that might sound controversial: this isn't your fault.

I mean that. Not in a therapeutic "let's make you feel better" way. I mean it as a factual observation about the world you're living in.

Jennifer eventually ended up at a budgeting workshop I taught at the Harold Washington Library downtown. Free workshop, Saturday morning, part of some adult education program the library was running. She didn't say much during the session, just took notes in a spiral notebook. But afterward she stayed, and we sat in those uncomfortable plastic library chairs for maybe twenty minutes looking at her bank statements together on her phone.

Not building a budget. Not setting goals. Just trying to figure out where the money was actually going.

You know what we found?

Nothing dramatic. No gambling problem. No secret shopping addiction. No buried trauma manifesting as retail therapy. No financial emergency, no crisis, no single big thing she could point to and say "ah, that's the problem."

Just a thousand invisible leaks.

A hundred and nineteen dollars a month to Equinox, a gym she'd visited maybe twice since signing up in January with the best intentions. Forty-seven for Headspace, a meditation app she'd downloaded during a particularly stressful week and then forgotten existed—she'd meditated maybe three times total. Fifteen for iCloud storage she didn't use because she'd upgraded her phone in November and the free tier was plenty now. Thirty-two for FabFitFun, one of those subscription boxes with artisanal whatever-the-hell, which had seemed charming when she signed up but now just created clutter in her apartment—unopened boxes stacked in the corner of her bedroom.

Eighty-nine dollars for her cell phone plan through Verizon when comparable plans at T-Mobile or Mint cost half that or less. She just hadn't bothered to call and negotiate because who has time for that? Who wants to spend forty-five minutes on hold and then argue with some customer retention specialist whose job is to wear you down?

These weren't conscious choices anymore. They were just *happening*. Autopay had turned them invisible. They were background noise. Elevator music for her bank account.

And then there was the daily stuff, the real stuff, the expenses that felt necessary in the moment and actually kind of were. Eight dollars for lunch because she worked twelve-hour shifts and didn't have time to pack anything, and honestly after dealing with people's actual health crises all morning the last thing she wanted to do was eat some sad desk salad she'd made on Sunday. Six for coffee because the hospital coffee tasted like it had been filtered through a gym sock and sitting for three hours. Twelve for dinner on her way home a few nights a week because after twelve hours on her feet, after dealing with someone's infected surgical wound and someone else's medication mixup and the family member who wouldn't stop asking questions she'd already answered twice, cooking felt impossible. Standing in her kitchen and chopping vegetables and waiting for things to heat felt like asking too much.

Individually? None of it seemed important. None of it felt like a budget crisis.

Who cares about six dollars? What's eight bucks for lunch when you're working a job that matters, when you're literally helping people survive?

Collectively? Over a month? Over a year?

It was running her life.

We added it up. Just the subscriptions she'd completely forgotten about, the ones she hadn't used in months, the ones that were just silently charging her card on the same day every month: three hundred and eighty-seven dollars. The daily convenience purchases—coffee, lunch, dinner a few times a week, the occasional smoothie on the way to work because she'd slept through her alarm and skipped breakfast: roughly six hundred and fifty.

That's over a thousand dollars flowing out of her life every single month on things she barely noticed, wouldn't miss if they disappeared tomorrow, and definitely didn't value when you actually asked her if they were worth it.

A thousand dollars a month. Twelve thousand a year.

Enough to say yes to being maid of honor without a second of panic. Enough to build an emergency fund. Enough to stop lying awake doing mental math about tire replacement.

But she didn't know. The money just left. Quietly. Automatically. Invisibly.

And that's the thing about cash flow—when you don't understand it, you're not making decisions about your money. Your money is making decisions about your life.

So why does this happen? And I mean really happen, mechanically happen, not the moralistic explanation where someone lectures you about personal responsibility and making better choices.

Why does this happen to smart, capable, financially responsible people who aren't idiots, who passed algebra, who can figure out a complicated subway system in a foreign country but can't figure out where their paycheck went?

You might be thinking: "Because people are careless. Because they don't pay attention. Because they're living beyond their means and not being honest about it."

And sure, sometimes. There's some of that. But mostly—and I mean this—mostly it happens because the entire system you're living in is specifically, intentionally, deliberately designed to make your spending invisible.

This isn't an accident. This is architecture.

Let me tell you about automatic payments first, because this is where the invisibility really starts.

I'm not saying autopay is evil—I use it myself, I recommend it for certain things, it's incredibly useful for making sure your rent actually gets paid and you don't get evicted because you forgot to mail a check—but it fundamentally changed the nature of spending. Changed it at a level most people don't think about.

Your gym membership renews. Your streaming services charge you. Your insurance deducts. Your phone bill processes. Your subscriptions for software you barely use and music you don't listen to and cloud storage you don't need—all of it happens while you're asleep, or at work, or living your actual life.

There's no moment where you consciously think, "Yes, I choose to spend money on this today."

There's no decision. It just happens.

And companies know this. They are deeply, financially invested in you forgetting about them. This is not speculation on my part—I've read the investor presentations, the quarterly earnings calls where executives literally talk about "reducing churn through frictionless auto-renewal." They know. They're counting on it.

That's why they make signing up frictionless and canceling annoying. That's why the cancellation process requires clicking through six different "Are you sure?" screens and sometimes—I am not making this up, this is real—calling a phone number during business hours and speaking to a human being whose actual job description is to talk you out of leaving.

"What if we gave you two months free?"

"What if we downgraded you to a cheaper tier?"

"Can I ask why you're canceling?"

On and on until you just give up and keep the subscription because it's easier than fighting.

They're counting on inertia. They're counting on you not noticing. They're counting on the eighteen dollars a month being just small enough that you won't bother to go through the hassle of canceling.

And it works. It works incredibly well. The entire subscription economy is built on people forgetting they're subscribed.

I did an informal survey once—not scientific, just asking people at workshops—about how many active subscriptions they thought they had versus how many they actually had when they checked. The average guess was around five or six. The average actual number when they went through their bank statements and credit card charges? Fourteen.

Fourteen separate recurring charges most people couldn't name off the top of their head.

Then there's the convenience economy, which has weaponized friction. Or rather, weaponized the *removal* of friction.

Every additional step between you and a purchase is friction—friction that gives you a moment to think, to reconsider, to decide whether you actually want this thing or you're just bored or stressed or trying to feel something.

Twenty years ago, buying something required work. You had to decide you wanted it, physically go to a store or at least find a catalog, find your wallet, pull out your credit card, hand it to someone, wait for them to run it through one of those old ka-chunk machines or type the number into a terminal, sign a receipt.

All those tiny steps, those little moments of inconvenience, created opportunities to think. "Do I really need this? Do I want it enough to go through all this hassle?"

Now? Tap. Done.

One-click ordering. Face ID. Apple Pay. Your card's already saved on every website you've ever visited. Amazon has your payment information stored and can deliver things to your house in two days, sometimes one day, sometimes same-day if you're in a major city. You don't even have to get off the couch.

Companies like Amazon have spent billions—and I mean billions, this is not hyperbole—of dollars removing every possible moment of friction because they know, because this is backed by actual behavioral research, that friction prevents purchases.

So they removed it. All of it.

You can buy something now before your conscious brain even registers that you're spending money. Before you've had time to think about whether you actually need a new pair of running shoes or you're just procrastinating on the thing you're supposed to be doing. Before you've considered whether you'll actually read that book or it'll just join the stack of unread books on your nightstand.

The purchase happens faster than thought.

And then there's cash. Or rather, the complete disappearance of cash from daily life.

There's real psychological research on this—studies going back decades, back when people actually used cash for things—showing that handing over physical bills creates a sense of loss that swiping a card doesn't. You watch the cash leave your hand. Your wallet gets physically lighter. You can see that you had six twenties this morning and now you have two. It's tangible. It's physical. It registers emotionally in a way that tapping a piece of plastic against a screen just doesn't.

But digital spending? Completely abstract. Just numbers on a screen going down. No physical sensation. No weight. No emotional register. You can spend two hundred dollars on a Friday night and feel almost nothing, just a vague awareness that you tapped your card a few times.

I tested this on myself once, deliberately, because I was curious whether the research held up in my own life. Withdrew three hundred dollars in cash at the beginning of a week and made myself use only cash for everything—coffee, lunch, groceries, everything. No cards.

It was almost painful. Physically uncomfortable.

Handing over a twenty for a twelve-dollar lunch and getting back a five and three ones and feeling how thin my wallet was getting. By Thursday I was rationing, making different choices, because the stack of bills was visibly shrinking and I didn't want to run out before the weekend.

The next week I went back to using my card for everything. Spent almost five hundred dollars and barely noticed. Same purchases, same habits, totally different emotional experience.

None of this makes you irresponsible. It doesn't make you bad with money. It makes you human.

You're living in a system specifically, intentionally designed to make spending invisible and painless and automatic. Of course you don't know where your money goes. The system doesn't *want* you to know. Companies have invested enormous amounts of money and research into making sure you don't know, because the moment you start paying attention is the moment you might stop spending.

There's another piece to this that nobody talks about, and it has to do with how we experience time.

Most budgeting advice treats money like it flows in and out on a neat monthly schedule. You get paid once a month—or twice a month, or every two weeks, whatever—and you spend money throughout the month, and at the end of the month you tally it up and see how you did.

But that's not how money actually moves through your life.

Money leaves in waves. Clusters. Unexpected bursts.

Your car insurance is due in February. Then nothing related to your car for five months except gas and maybe an oil change. Then in July your registration is due. Then in August you need new tires because the tread's finally worn down and you've been putting it off but you can't anymore. Then nothing until December when you need to renew your AAA membership.

Your subscriptions all hit on different days. Netflix on the third. Spotify on the seventh. Your cell phone on the twelfth. Your internet bill on the fifteenth. The gym on the twentieth. None of them aligned, none of them coordinated, just this steady drip of charges throughout the month that you can't see coming because they're scattered.

And then there are the expenses that aren't predictable at all. Your friend's wedding. Your sister's baby shower. The birthday dinner for your coworker that somehow costs sixty dollars because the restaurant split the bill evenly and you only had a salad but other people ordered three cocktails each and now you're subsidizing their alcohol. The vet bill when your cat stops eating and you panic. The new phone because you dropped the old one and the screen shattered and yes you could probably get it fixed for eighty bucks but you've been meaning to upgrade anyway and the new model is only thirty dollars a month for twenty-four months which doesn't sound like that much except it's seven hundred and twenty dollars total but you don't think about it that way in the moment.

This is what your actual cash flow looks like. Not a smooth, predictable curve. A jagged mess of spikes and valleys that you can't anticipate and can't plan for unless you can actually see them.

And most people can't see them because most budgeting tools aren't built for this. They're built for the fantasy version of money where everything is monthly and predictable and stable.

I learned this the hard way—not from my own finances, honestly, but from watching other people struggle with systems that should have worked but didn't.

Marcus was an accountant. An actual accountant, someone who worked with numbers and spreadsheets and financial statements for a living, someone you'd think would have this completely figured out. He came to one of my workshops because even though he understood budgets intellectually, even though he could build complex financial models for his clients, he couldn't make his own budget work.

He'd tried Mint. He'd tried YNAB. He'd tried building his own spreadsheet with formulas and conditional formatting and charts that updated automatically. All of it failed for the same reason: the systems required constant attention. Daily logging. Categorizing transactions. Reconciling accounts. Adjusting projections.

And he'd do it for a while. A week, maybe two. Then he'd have a busy week at work—tax season, audit season, whatever—and he'd fall behind. Then he'd feel guilty about falling behind, which made him avoid opening the app, which made him fall further behind, which increased the guilt, until eventually he'd just abandon the whole thing and start over with a new system and the cycle would repeat.

The problem wasn't Marcus. The problem was that the systems were demanding more attention than the problem was worth. They were optimized for precision, not for reality.

So what's the actual fix here? What do you do with this information?

Because I can already hear some of you thinking: "Great. The system is designed against me. Companies are trying to make me spend. My cash flow is chaotic and unpredictable. Cool. Very helpful. What am I supposed to do about it?"

Fair question.

Here's the thing most budgeting books won't tell you: you don't need to track every dollar. You don't need perfect precision. You don't need a color-coded spreadsheet with sixteen categories and subcategories and a dashboard that updates in real-time.

You need *enough* visibility to make better decisions.

That's it. That's the actual bar.

Not perfect tracking. Not comprehensive analysis. Just enough clarity to see where the big leaks are so you can decide—consciously, deliberately—whether those leaks are worth it.

Think about it like a health checkup. When you go to the doctor for a routine physical, they don't measure every single biomarker in your body. They don't track every hormone, every enzyme, every cell count. They check the big ones. Blood pressure. Cholesterol. Blood sugar. Heart rate. A few key indicators that tell them whether things are generally okay or whether something needs attention.

That's what we're doing here. Not a comprehensive financial autopsy. Just a basic health check.

And the beautiful thing—the thing that makes this actually work for people who've failed at every other budgeting system—is that you don't need a lot of precision to get massive clarity.

You don't need to know you spent exactly eight dollars and forty-seven cents on coffee last Tuesday. You need to know you're spending something like one hundred and fifty to two hundred bucks a month on coffee and whether that feels worth it to you.

You don't need to track every individual grocery trip. You need to know you're spending roughly five to six hundred a month on food and whether that's reasonable given how you eat and where you shop and how often you're cooking versus ordering delivery.

Rough categories. Rough numbers. Enough to see the shape of your cash flow without drowning in data.

Here's how this actually works in practice.

You're going to look at one month of spending. Just one. Not six months, not a year, not some averaged projection. One month. Preferably last month, because it's recent and you can still remember what happened and the numbers are real, not hypothetical.

Pull up your bank account. Your credit card statements. Any other accounts where money regularly leaves. You're going to scroll through and you're going to put every expense into one of these buckets:

Fixed essentials. Rent. Mortgage. Car payment. Insurance. Student loans. Utilities. The stuff that's the same every month, that you can't really avoid, that would cause serious problems if you stopped paying. You're not making decisions about these right now—you're just acknowledging they exist and naming how much they cost.

Variable essentials. Groceries. Gas. Prescriptions. Basic household supplies. The stuff you need to survive and function but that varies month to month based on what you use and what you buy. Again, not trying to optimize these yet. Just seeing them.

Subscriptions and recurring charges. Everything that auto-bills. Streaming services. Apps. Memberships. Software. Cloud storage. Subscription boxes. The stuff that happens automatically whether you use it or not.

Discretionary daily spending. Coffee. Lunch out. Dinner out. Drinks. The small purchases that add up. The daily friction points.

Occasional big stuff. Clothes. Electronics. Furniture. Gifts. Travel. The irregular expenses that don't happen every month but still matter.

That's it. Five buckets. You don't need twenty categories. You don't need to distinguish between "groceries" and "household supplies" or between "entertainment" and "dining out." You need enough separation to see patterns without enough complexity to make you quit.

Go through last month. Put every expense in a bucket. Add up the buckets. Write down the totals.

This should take you maybe ten minutes. Fifteen if you're being thorough. Not an hour. Not daily maintenance. One short session.

And here's what you're looking for: surprises.

Not judgment. Not shame. Surprises.

Which number is higher than you expected? Which bucket made you go "wait, really?" when you added it up?

For Jennifer, it was subscriptions and daily spending. She knew she had some subscriptions, but seeing three hundred and eighty-seven dollars in charges for things she'd completely forgotten about was visceral. Same with the six hundred and fifty in daily convenience purchases—individually they'd felt like nothing, but collectively they were more than her car payment.

For Marcus, the accountant, it was occasional big stuff. He'd been unconsciously smoothing it in his head, thinking of it as small and infrequent, but when he actually added up the clothes and the electronics and the gifts and the weekend trips, it was averaging close to a thousand dollars a month. More than his rent.

That moment of surprise—that "oh, huh" moment when the number doesn't match your mental model—is the entire point of this exercise.

Because once you see it, once you've made the invisible visible, you can decide whether it's worth it.

Not whether it's good or bad. Not whether some financial guru would approve. Whether *you* think it's worth it given your actual priorities and your actual life.

Maybe those subscriptions aren't worth it. Maybe you genuinely forgot about half of them and you'd be just as happy without them and that's nearly four hundred dollars a month you could redirect somewhere more meaningful.

Or maybe the daily coffee is absolutely worth it. Maybe that six dollars every morning is the small moment of pleasure that makes your commute bearable, and you'd rather cut something else than give that up. Fine. Great. It's your money. But now it's a conscious choice instead of an invisible leak.

You might be wondering: "Okay, but what about the chaotic timing? What about the fact that my car insurance hits in February and my registration hits in July and none of this is evenly distributed?"

Good question. You're paying attention.

Here's the trick: you're not budgeting month-to-month anymore. You're budgeting in averages.

Take all those occasional expenses—the ones that don't happen every month but still happen regularly—and divide them by twelve. Car insurance is four hundred every six months? That's sixty-six dollars a month on average. Annual Amazon Prime membership is one hundred and forty? That's about twelve bucks a month. Holiday gifts usually run you around six hundred in December? Fifty a month.

You're not going to spend exactly sixty-six dollars on car insurance every month. Obviously. It's going to be zero for five months and then four hundred in month six. But if you think of it as sixty-six a month, if you mentally allocate that amount even in the months when you're not actually paying it, you won't be surprised when the bill comes.

This is the concept behind the envelope system we're going to build in the next chapter, but you don't need the full system yet to start thinking this way. You just need to shift from "what am I spending this month" to "what am I spending on average over time."

Because that's how you actually smooth out the chaos. Not by pretending everything happens monthly, but by averaging the irregular stuff into regular mental buckets so you can plan for it.

Let me tell you what happened with Jennifer after we sat in that library and looked at her numbers.

She didn't build a complicated budget. She didn't set up a bunch of rules or restrictions. She didn't download an app or create a spreadsheet or start tracking every transaction.

She just canceled the subscriptions she'd forgotten about. Took maybe twenty minutes. She called Verizon and threatened to switch to T-Mobile and they magically found her a plan that was thirty dollars cheaper. She kept the daily coffee—decided that was worth it—but started packing lunch a few times a week because it turned out she didn't actually value the eight-dollar salad from the hospital cafeteria, she was just defaulting to it because it was easy.

That was it. Those were the only changes she made.

Three months later, she had almost two thousand dollars in her savings account. Money that used to just evaporate had started sticking around because she'd made a few invisible leaks visible and then made conscious choices about which ones to plug.

She told me she slept better. That was the phrase she used: "I sleep better now."

Not because she'd achieved some perfect financial state. Not because she'd maxed out her retirement contributions or built a six-month emergency fund or hit some arbitrary savings goal.

Because she wasn't lying awake at 4 AM doing mental math anymore. Because when her friend asked her to be in the wedding, her first emotion was joy instead of panic. Because she finally felt like she was making decisions about her money instead of her money making decisions about her life.

That's what understanding your cash flow actually gets you.

Not a perfect budget. Not financial enlightenment. Not some guru's approval.

Clarity. Agency. The ability to make conscious choices about how you want to live instead of just reacting to wherever the money happens to flow.

So here's what I want you to do this week. Not eventually. Not when you feel motivated. This week.

Pick one hour. Any hour. Put it on your calendar if that helps. You're going to sit down with your bank account and your credit card statements from last month—just last month, we're not doing a historical deep dive—and you're going to categorize your spending into those five buckets I mentioned earlier.

Fixed essentials. Variable essentials. Subscriptions and recurring charges. Discretionary daily spending. Occasional big stuff.

Every expense goes in a bucket. Add up each bucket. Write down the totals.

Then look at them. Just look. Don't judge, don't fix, don't optimize. Just notice which numbers surprise you. Which ones are higher than you expected. Which ones make you go "huh."

And then—this is the important part, don't skip this—pick one leak. Just one. The one that surprised you most, or that you value least, or that just bugs you when you see it written down as an actual number instead of invisible background noise.

And plug it.

Cancel the subscription you forgot about. Call your phone company and negotiate a lower rate. Pack lunch twice next week instead of buying it. Whatever feels like the most obvious, easiest, lowest-friction fix based on what you just discovered.

One leak. One plug. That's it.

We're not doing a complete financial overhaul. We're not building the whole system yet. That comes in Chapter Three. Right now, we're just proving to yourself that visibility creates options. That seeing where your money goes gives you the power to change where it goes.

Because the real insight here—the thing that changes everything once you really get it—is that most people are flying blind. They have no idea where their money is going. They feel broke on decent incomes because thousands of dollars are leaking out in ways they can't see and didn't consciously choose.

You're not going to be that person anymore.

You're going to look. You're going to see. And you're going to start making actual decisions instead of just letting the system make decisions for you.

The numbers are already there, in your account, waiting for you to look at them. One hour. Five buckets. One surprise. One fix.

Do that, and you'll understand something that most people never figure out: you don't need perfect control over every dollar to change your financial life. You just need to know where the big leaks are.

And now you know how to find them.

...tap to pay, grab drink, leave.

She tapped the screen again, scrolling past notifications she didn't have time to read, wondering if anyone else felt this constant low-level anxiety about money disappearing into thin air.

Chapter 3: Building Your Envelope System

My grandmother never balanced a checkbook in her life. Every Friday when my grandfather came home from the die-cast factory, she'd meet him at the door, take his paycheck, and walk straight to the kitchen table where a stack of white envelopes waited—the cheap kind from Woolworth's, already wrinkled from being reused month after month, some of them labeled in her careful cursive: *Groceries. Gas. Electric. Church.*

The cash got divided before anything else happened. Before she thought about whether they could afford a movie that weekend. Before my grandfather eyed the new power drill at Sears. Before any want got anywhere near that money. Each envelope got its share and then got tucked into the kitchen drawer.

When the grocery envelope was empty, you ate what was in the pantry. No exceptions. No mental gymnastics about borrowing from the gas envelope to cover this week's splurge at the store—the gas money was in a different envelope, three feet away in that same drawer, and touching it meant the car didn't move next week.

She died with zero debt and a paid-off house on a factory worker's income in a town where half their neighbors had declared bankruptcy at least once.

I'm not suggesting we all start stuffing cash in kitchen drawers—though there's something appealing about that level of simplicity. But the *principle* she used, physical separation of money by purpose, worked because it made the invisible visible. That's exactly what most of us are missing when we check our bank app and see one big number staring back at us, representing everything and therefore nothing.

Here's what that one big number actually costs you, and I mean this literally, not as some abstract financial concept.

You're in the grocery store. Your kid is melting down in the cart because you said no to the cereal with the cartoon character. Someone's waiting behind you in line, close enough that you can hear them breathing, and you can feel their impatience radiating into your back. You're holding the good coffee—the one you actually like, the one that makes Monday mornings slightly less brutal, the one with the blue bag that costs twelve dollars instead of seven—and you're doing real-time calculus in your head. What's in the account right now. What bills are hitting this week. What you've already spent on groceries this trip. Did the insurance payment clear yet or is that still pending. Did your partner stop for gas yesterday or was that last week.

You *think* you have enough. Pretty sure. But you're not certain, because that number in your checking account represents this week's groceries and next month's rent and your phone bill and the birthday gift you still need to buy and that streaming service that auto-renewed yesterday and you're trying to hold all of it in your head at once while your kid is screaming and the line is building and your brain is already tired from the eight other decisions you made today.

So you put back the good coffee. You grab the store brand. Not because you can't afford the twelve-dollar bag. Because you don't actually *know* what you can afford, and the uncertainty makes you choose the safe option every single time.

That constant low-grade anxiety about whether each individual purchase is okay? That's not coming from not having enough money. It's coming from not knowing what any of that money is *for*. And it's exhausting in a way that's hard to explain to someone who hasn't felt it, this grinding decision fatigue that follows you through every store, every restaurant menu, every "should we go out this weekend or stay home" conversation with your partner where neither of you wants to be the one to say we can't afford it but neither of you is quite sure we can.

The envelope system fixes this, and I want to be clear about something before we go further: it doesn't fix it by being sophisticated or clever. It fixes it by being almost embarrassingly simple.

The basic mechanics are this. You take your money and divide it into categories that mirror how you actually spend: groceries, gas, rent, entertainment, whatever matches your real life. Historically—and by historically I mean my grandmother's generation and every generation before that—people did this with actual physical envelopes and cash. Fifty dollars in the "date night" envelope at the start of the month. Two hundred in "groceries." Seventy-five in "gas." When the envelope was empty, that spending stopped until next month.

The beauty wasn't the envelopes themselves. It was the psychological shift that happened when abstract money became concrete.

A grocery budget stopped being a line item you'd update later in some spreadsheet you were definitely going to maintain this time, really, you promised yourself. It became actual bills in your hand, shrinking with every trip to the store. You could *see* the money leaving. You could feel the thickness of the stack getting thinner. Your brain, which evolved to understand physical objects and has a hard time with abstract numbers on screens, suddenly got it.

Sarah—the nurse from Chapter 1 who was spending $600 a month on takeout without realizing it—switched to cash envelopes for her "eating out" category after we talked through her numbers. She pulled $300 in twenties from the ATM on the first of the month, stuck them in an envelope in her purse, and made herself a rule: when it's gone, it's gone.

She called me three weeks later. "It's weird," she said, "but physically handing over a twenty-dollar bill makes me pause in ways that swiping a card never did. The card feels infinite. Like it's connected to some bottomless well of money that'll just... work itself out somehow. The cash feels finite. I can see it disappearing."

That first month she cut her takeout spending by forty percent. Not because she was suffering or white-knuckling her way through deprivation. Because she could *see* what each decision cost. The visibility changed everything. By month three, she told me, she wasn't even thinking about it anymore—the habit had shifted. She'd become the kind of person who meal-prepped on Sundays (something she'd always thought sounded exhausting and joyless) because seeing that stack of bills shrink made the consequences real in a way a bank balance never had.

Now I know what you're thinking, because I thought it too: carrying around envelopes full of cash in 2026 sounds impractical at best, genuinely unsafe at worst. You're right. I tried it myself for exactly one month in 2019 as an experiment, stuffing my wallet with a few hundred dollars in various denominations, and the anxiety of carrying that much cash around outweighed any benefit. Plus, half the places I needed to buy things didn't even take cash anymore. The coffee shop near my office went cashless in 2020. My gym doesn't have a register, just an app. The farmer's market near me—which you'd think would be old-school enough for cash—has Venmo QR codes on every stall.

But here's what matters: the *principle* works. Physical separation creates psychological clarity. We just need to recreate that principle digitally, and it turns out that's not actually that hard.

There are apps designed specifically for this. Qube Money is one—it links to your bank account and lets you create digital "buckets" for each spending category. You fund each bucket at the beginning of the month, and when you make a purchase, the app deducts it from the appropriate bucket. You get the psychological benefit of watching that specific pool of money shrink without the logistical nightmare of managing physical cash. YNAB—You Need A Budget—works on a similar concept, though with a slightly different philosophy about how money flows between categories. Goodbudget is another option, designed to mimic the physical envelope method as closely as possible. New apps appear regularly, each with slightly different approaches to the same basic idea.

But you don't actually *need* an app to make this work, and I want to emphasize this because the app thing stops a lot of people before they even start. They download something, get overwhelmed by the interface, abandon it in the setup phase when it asks them to categorize three months of past transactions, and assume the whole envelope concept isn't for them. The app is just a tool. The principle is what matters. You can achieve the same result with nothing more than your existing bank account, a simple spreadsheet or even a piece of paper, and the discipline to check your running totals before you spend.

I'll show you exactly how in a minute, but first I want you to see what this actually looks like when someone implements it in real life, with real numbers and real complications, because the theory is useless if you can't see how it survives contact with reality.

Meet David and Emily. Early thirties. Two young kids, four and two. Combined monthly income of $6,000 after taxes. David worked as an assistant manager at a regional hardware chain, the kind of place where he knew most of the regulars by name and could tell you which brand of deck screws would hold up best in treated lumber. Emily did medical billing from home three days a week so she could be around for the kids—the two-year-old hadn't started daycare yet and the four-year-old was only in preschool part-time.

They weren't in crisis. They paid their bills on time. Had a roof over their heads, food in the fridge. Their kids wore clothes that fit and had toys they didn't need but got anyway because what kind of childhood doesn't have toys. They weren't drowning.

But every month, money just... vanished.

They'd get to the end of the month with maybe a hundred bucks left, sometimes less, and neither of them could really explain where it all went. They weren't taking vacations. They weren't buying anything big—no new furniture, no new car, nothing that would show up as an obvious leak when you looked at their bank statements. It was just... gone. Absorbed into the general noise of living. Swallowed by a thousand small decisions that seemed fine in the moment.

Emily reached out to me in March of last year. "I feel like we make decent money," she wrote in an email at eleven at night when both kids were finally asleep and she had a minute to think. "But we're always broke and I don't understand why. We're not idiots. We're not out buying jet skis. Where is it all *going*?"

I hear this question a lot, phrased different ways but with the same bewildered frustration underneath. People who make good money, who aren't reckless, who consider themselves reasonably responsible, and yet somehow money disappears like water through their fingers and they have no idea where the leak is.

The answer is almost never one big leak. It's a hundred tiny ones.

Their first step was tracking a full month of spending. Not estimating, not guessing, not relying on their general sense of things. Actually writing down every single expense as it happened. Every coffee. Every grocery run. Every impulse buy at Target while picking up diapers because Target is designed by psychological warfare experts who know exactly how to get you to leave with forty dollars of things you didn't come for.

This part is tedious. I'm not going to pretend otherwise. It requires you to save receipts or check your bank app multiple times a day or use one of those tracking apps that links to your accounts. It feels fussy and excessive, especially in the moment when you just want to buy the thing and move on with your day.

But you only have to do it once—one month of obsessive tracking to get the baseline data. After that, you'll know your patterns well enough that you can work from estimates. One month. Thirty days of mild annoyance in exchange for finally knowing where your money actually goes.

Here's what David and Emily found when the month was over:

Housing: $1,800 Utilities: $350 Groceries: $700 Dining out: $400 Transportation: $500 Childcare: $600 Debt payments: $750 (a car loan and some lingering credit card debt from when Emily was on unpaid maternity leave two years ago and they'd put groceries on plastic for three months) Entertainment: $200 Miscellaneous: $200

Total: $5,500.

That left $500 unaccounted for.

Five hundred dollars a month that just... disappeared into the void. Impulse purchases, mostly. A toy here because the kid threw a fit in the store and David was too exhausted to fight it. A nicer bottle of wine there because they'd had a rough week. That thing on Amazon that seemed essential at the time—what even was it? Emily scrolled back through their order history and couldn't remember half the purchases from two weeks ago. A phone charger cable because the old one was fraying. A set of food storage containers because the old ones were stained and it was bothering her. A book someone recommended in a podcast. Replaceable things that probably weren't creating any lasting value in their lives.

None of it memorable. All of it adding up.

And here's what I want you to notice about their reaction, because it's important. When Emily saw that $500 line, her first instinct was shame. "I felt like an idiot," she told me. "Like, how did we not *know* we were bleeding that much money? What's wrong with us?"

Nothing is wrong with you if you're having the same reaction right now to your own numbers. The system is designed to hide this from you. One big account balance. Purchases that feel small in isolation. No friction, no visibility, just swipe and go and trust that it'll all work out somehow.

Your brain isn't equipped to track dozens of micro-transactions across multiple categories without help. You're not failing at something you should naturally be good at. You're trying to do something humans have never had to do before in history—manage purely abstract money with zero physical constraints.

Once they saw the actual numbers laid out, the path forward became obvious. They didn't need to slash their lifestyle or move to a cheaper apartment or sell the car. They needed to make *intentional* choices instead of passive ones. They needed to stop letting money happen *to* them and start telling it where to go.

They started with the easy wins—or what looked like easy wins on paper. Dining out felt like the biggest leak. Four hundred dollars a month on restaurants and takeout. And here's the thing Emily told me that stuck with me: they weren't even *enjoying* most of it.

Tuesday night pizza because they were both too tired to cook and the kids needed to eat something. Drive-through breakfast on Saturday because they were running late to the four-year-old's tumbling class and nobody had time for anything else. Sunday brunch because that's just what they did, it was the routine, and routines are comforting even when they're expensive. None of it was creating memories or joy. It was just convenient calories, purchased during moments of decision fatigue when cooking felt like too much.

They cut that category in half. Two hundred dollars a month for dining out, which meant choosing their restaurant trips carefully, making them actually *count*. Real date nights when Emily's mom could watch the kids, not exhaustion nights. Brunch when they actually wanted it and had time to enjoy it, not because the calendar said Sunday and they couldn't think of anything else.

Entertainment dropped from $200 to $100. They realized they were paying for three streaming services they rarely used. David would watch baseball highlights on YouTube anyway—he didn't need the full MLB package that auto-renewed every April and that he'd forgotten he even had. Emily had only opened Hulu twice in the past month to watch a show everyone said she *had* to see but honestly wasn't that into. They were also saying yes to every kid birthday party and weekend activity without considering the cost. Little Brayden's trampoline park party? Thirty bucks. That Saturday pumpkin patch outing the preschool organized? Forty-five. The kids were four and two—they'd be just as happy at the free playground down the street, and they wouldn't remember the difference five years from now.

Trimming entertainment didn't mean eliminating fun. It meant being selective, choosing what mattered.

That freed up $300 right there. They found another $100 by simply being more mindful about impulse purchases—implementing a 24-hour rule for anything over twenty dollars that wasn't on the grocery list. If they still wanted it the next day, fine. But most of the time the urge passed. The Amazon cart that looked essential at eleven PM looked silly in the morning light.

Total freed up: $400 per month.

Here's where it gets interesting, and this is the part that separates people who succeed with this from people who burn out in six weeks and go back to their old patterns. They didn't just sock all that money away in savings and feel virtuous. They didn't try to be heroes. They split it strategically.

Two hundred toward extra debt payments, accelerating their timeline to be debt-free. A hundred fifty into a dedicated savings account for a family vacation they actually wanted to take—David had been talking about taking the kids to see the Grand Canyon since the four-year-old got old enough to appreciate it, and now they were actually working toward it instead of just wishing.

And the remaining fifty? They split it. Twenty-five dollars a month in "fun money" for each of them individually. Money they could blow on whatever they wanted without judgment or explanation from the other person. David bought comic books he'd never read. Emily got the good coffee at the fancy place downtown instead of making it at home. It was theirs, no questions asked, and that mattered more than you'd think.

Because here's what kills most budgets: the feeling that you're being punished. That you've lost all agency. That every dollar is spoken for and you're just a robot executing someone else's plan for your life. The personal spending money, even though it was small, gave them back a sense of freedom. They were choosing this system. It wasn't being imposed on them.

Their new envelope allocations looked like this:

Housing: $1,800 Utilities: $350 Groceries: $700 Dining out: $200 Transportation: $500 Childcare: $600 Debt payments: $950 Entertainment: $100 Vacation fund: $150 Personal spending (David): $25 Personal spending (Emily): $25 Miscellaneous buffer: $350

Notice that buffer category at the end. This is the thing I need you to understand, because it's where most budgets fall apart in the real world and people blame themselves instead of blaming the plan.

Life doesn't care about your budget. Tires go flat on Tuesday morning when you're already running late. Kids spike fevers and need the urgent care co-pay. Friends have babies and you need to buy a gift unless you're planning to show up empty-handed like a sociopath. The dishwasher dies and you need to at least get it looked at even if you end up just running it with a broken latch for six months like we did. The dog eats something stupid and needs the emergency vet. Your partner's childhood friend is getting married and you can't just not go to the wedding.

If you don't build in a buffer—somewhere around five to ten percent of your total income—the first unexpected expense will blow up your whole system. You'll have to steal from another envelope to cover it, and then that category will be short, and you'll feel like the budget failed. You'll feel like *you* failed. And you'll abandon the whole thing and go back to the anxious checking-your-balance-before-every-purchase life you were trying to escape.

The buffer isn't pessimism. It's realism. It's acknowledging that you don't have perfect information about what this month will throw at you, and that's okay, you've planned for it. When something unexpected happens—and it will—you're not derailing the plan. You're executing the part of the plan designed for exactly this situation.

Emily told me that the first month felt restrictive. Like they were being punished for past mistakes. She'd check the dining-out envelope on the 15th and see they'd already spent $140 of their $200 budget and feel this creeping sense of deprivation setting in. "We can't even get pizza?"

But by month two, something shifted. She described it as finally being able to *breathe*.

Not because they suddenly had more money—they didn't, they had the same $6,000 they'd always had. Because they finally knew exactly what they could spend without guilt or anxiety. The decision was already made. The money was already allocated. She didn't have to wonder or calculate or stress.

When she wanted to take the kids to a movie on a rainy Saturday, she checked the entertainment envelope. Forty dollars left for the month, and it was only the 12th. Okay. Movie night happens at home this time. They'd make popcorn, build a blanket fort, turn it into a thing. The four-year-old would remember the fort more than she'd remember the theater anyway.

No drama, no guilt, no desperate mental math trying to figure out if they could "afford" it in some abstract sense. The envelope was nearly empty. Decision made.

And then—this is the part she said changed everything—she could *relax* for the rest of the month because she'd already made the hard choice. The decision was done. She wasn't carrying it around in the back of her mind, wondering if she should have said yes, wondering if saying no made her a bad mom, wondering if they were being too restrictive or not restrictive enough.

That's the real power of this system, and I need you to understand this because it's not what most people expect going in. It's not about restriction. It's about *removing the anxiety of constant decision-making*.

You decide once—at the beginning of the month, in one focused session when you're clear-headed and looking at the big picture—where your money goes. Then you just follow the plan. Your willpower isn't being slowly drained by hundreds of tiny spending decisions every week. You're not standing in every store doing mental calculus, trying to figure out if this purchase is okay. You already know the answer. You decided it two weeks ago when you set up your envelopes.

The decision fatigue disappears. And it turns out that was most of the problem.

By month four, Emily said they'd stopped thinking about the budget as a separate thing they had to manage. It had become the water they swam in. She knew, without having to check, roughly how much was left in each category at any point in the month. Not because she was obsessively tracking—she checked maybe once a week—but because the boundaries had become internalized. She'd developed an intuitive sense of what they could and couldn't do, the same way my grandmother knew exactly how thick the stack in the grocery envelope was without having to count it.

Now let's talk about how you actually build this for yourself, because David and Emily's numbers aren't your numbers. Their life isn't your life. You might not have kids. You might not have debt. You might make twice what they make or half. The framework is the same, but the details have to be yours.

Start by listing every single expense from last month. Every. Single. One.

The big ones are easy—rent or mortgage, car payment, insurance. Those show up in your bank statement as obvious recurring charges with the same amount every month. But don't skip the small stuff just because it feels tedious to write down. That four-dollar coffee. The twelve-dollar streaming service you forgot you signed up for. The seven-dollar impulse buy at the checkout line because they put candy there on purpose and you were hungry and tired. The fifteen dollars you gave your kid for the school fundraiser. The six dollars you spent on parking because you were running late. The three-dollar ATM fee because you used the wrong bank. It all counts.

Grab your bank statements, your credit card bills, any receipts you've managed to save. If you use multiple cards or accounts, you'll need to check all of them—money has a way of spreading across accounts like water finding cracks. If you're missing data, estimate conservatively, but know that you'll need to track more carefully going forward to get accurate numbers.

And if you're like most people, looking at a full month of unfiltered spending is going to be mildly horrifying. That's fine. That's actually good. The horror is information. The discomfort you're feeling right now is the gap between what you *thought* you were spending and what you *actually* spent, and that gap is exactly what we're trying to close.

Now categorize everything. Start with these common categories and adjust based on your real life:

Housing — rent or mortgage, property tax if you pay it separately, HOA fees if you're cursed with those

Utilities — electric, water, gas, internet, phone (if you're still paying for a landline I want to know why, but also add it here)

Transportation — car payment, insurance, gas, maintenance, tolls, parking, public transit passes

Food — and this is important—split into *groceries* and *eating out*. Keep these separate. They feel like the same category because they're both food, but psychologically they're completely different spending patterns and you need to see them clearly. Groceries are planned. Eating out is often decision fatigue or convenience or social, and it behaves differently in your budget.

Personal care — haircuts, toiletries, prescriptions, doctor co-pays, gym membership

Entertainment — streaming services, hobbies, going out, concerts, sports, books, that thing you do to convince yourself life isn't just work and sleep

Debt payments — credit cards, student loans, personal loans, medical debt, anything where you owe someone money and they want it back

Savings — emergency fund, specific goals, retirement contributions if they're not already coming out of your paycheck

Don't be afraid to get more specific if it helps you see patterns. Maybe you realize you're spending a shocking amount on coffee specifically, not just "food" generally—make it its own category for a month so you can see it. Maybe you've got a hobby that's eating more money than you realized—pull it out of "entertainment" and give it its own line.

The categories should match how you actually spend, not how some budgeting book says you *should* spend. If you don't have a car, you don't need a transportation category (though you might need a bigger public transit line). If you don't have debt, lucky you, skip that one. If you've got three kids in sports, you might need a whole category just for "activities and equipment and the snack bar and the endless tournament fees."

Once you've got your spending categorized, add it all up. Then compare it to your income.

If the spending is less than the income—great. You've got room to work with. If the spending is more than the income—well, now you know why you feel broke all the time. You're spending more than you make, and that gap is getting covered by credit cards or overdraft fees or that slowly dwindling savings account you've been pretending not to notice.

Either way, you now have real data instead of vague anxiety. And real data can be worked with.

Look for the categories that surprised you. The ones where you thought "there's no way we spend that much on X" and then the numbers showed you that yes, actually, you do. Those are your opportunities.

Here's where most budget advice goes wrong. It tells you to cut everything. Skip the coffee. Cancel the streaming services. Stop eating out entirely. Cook every meal from dried beans and rice. Suffer now so you can thrive later.

That works for approximately nobody, and the people it does work for are the kind of people who'd succeed with any system because they've got unusual levels of willpower or desperation or both.

For the rest of us, the sustainable path is to cut the things that aren't actually creating value and *keep* the things that matter. Emily and David didn't eliminate dining out. They cut it in half and made the remaining meals count. They didn't cancel all their subscriptions. They kept the one they actually used and dumped the ones they'd forgotten about.

The goal isn't to punish yourself into financial stability. It's to align your spending with what you actually value, and stop wasting money on things that don't matter to you. Once you see where the money's going, that alignment becomes obvious.

Take the money you've freed up and assign it to your goals. More debt payments. Emergency fund. That vacation you've been talking about for three years. Whatever matters to you. But—and this is important—leave yourself some unstructured money. That buffer category for the unexpected, and some personal spending money that's truly yours to waste if you want to.

Now set up your envelopes. If you're using an app like Qube or YNAB, follow their setup process—they'll walk you through creating categories and assigning dollar amounts. If you're doing this manually, open a simple spreadsheet or grab a notebook. List each category, write the monthly allocation next to it, and commit to checking your running total before you spend.

On the first of the month, every dollar in your account gets assigned to an envelope. Not literally—it's all still sitting in your checking account, you're just tracking which dollars are for what purpose. When you buy groceries, you deduct from the grocery envelope. When you fill up the tank, you deduct from transportation. You're creating the psychological separation my grandmother had with her physical envelopes, just without the cash.

You might be wondering how this is different from just... knowing what your budget is and trying to stick to it. Fair question. The difference is the forced visibility and the hard boundaries.

When everything lives in one account and you just try to "be good" about spending, there's always wiggle room. Always a way to rationalize that this purchase is fine, you'll make up for it later, it's not that much, you deserve it after the week you've had. The envelope system removes the wiggle room. The grocery money is the grocery money. If it's gone on the 23rd, you're eating pantry meals for a week. That clarity—that hard boundary—changes behavior in ways that soft intentions never do.

The first month will feel strange. You'll probably mess up the tracking. You'll forget to log a purchase and then panic when your envelope doesn't match your bank account. You'll realize you allocated too little to one category and too much to another. That's fine. That's information. Adjust for next month.

By month three, it'll feel normal. You'll have a sense of the rhythm. You'll know which categories you over-estimated and which ones you under-estimated. You'll know whether you're someone who needs to check your envelopes daily or if once a week is enough.

And somewhere around month four or five, you'll have the experience Emily described. You'll be standing in a store, looking at something you want, and instead of that anxious "can we afford this" calculation, you'll just... know. You'll check the envelope—mentally or literally—and the answer will be clear. Yes, there's room. Or no, that money is spoken for. The decision will already be made. And you'll be able to walk away or make the purchase without guilt or second-guessing or that nagging voice in the back of your head wondering if you just made a mistake.

That's what we're building toward. Not perfection. Not some pristine budget that never gets touched. A system that makes the invisible visible, removes the constant low-grade anxiety of not knowing if spending is okay, and gives you back the mental energy you've been burning on hundreds of tiny financial decisions every week.

The question isn't whether the envelope system works—it does, it's worked for generations, the psychology is sound. The question is whether you're willing to spend one focused hour this weekend setting it up, and then five minutes a week maintaining it. Because if you are, the constant background hum of financial anxiety you've been living with can actually stop. Not someday when you make more money or finally get that promotion or win the lottery. This month. With the money you already have.

But knowing how to set up envelopes is only half the picture. The other half is knowing how *many* envelopes to create, and that's where most people either create a beautifully detailed system they'll abandon in two weeks, or a too-simple system that doesn't actually capture their spending. There's a sweet spot, a specific number of categories that's detailed enough to be useful but simple enough to maintain, and that's exactly what we're covering next.

The magic number sits somewhere between four and twelve categories. I know that's a range, not an answer, but stick with me because where *you* land in that range depends on one thing: whether adding another category makes your life easier or harder.

Here's how to find out.

Start with the absolute non-negotiables. These are the categories that exist whether you like it or not because the bill shows up every month. Rent or mortgage. Utilities. Phone. Insurance. Transportation—whether that's a car payment, gas, or a transit pass. Minimum debt payments if you're carrying any. Groceries. Those are your foundation categories, and most people end up with five to seven of them.

Now comes the interesting part. Everything else in your budget falls into one of two buckets: things you buy regularly enough that they deserve their own envelope, and things you buy so rarely they can share space with similar purchases.

Let's say you spend money on coffee shops three times a week. That's roughly twelve times a month. Does "coffee" need its own envelope, separate from "dining out" or "groceries"? Maybe. If you've been beating yourself up about coffee spending and you want to give yourself a specific amount to spend guilt-free, then yes, make it its own thing. If coffee spending doesn't stress you and you're fine lumping it in with food or entertainment, then no, it doesn't need its own line.

Same logic applies to everything else. Do you buy books often enough that "books" should be separate from "entertainment"? Do you spend on pet supplies regularly enough that it needs its own envelope, or can it fold into "household"? The answer isn't universal. It's personal. And it changes based on what you're trying to track or control.

The trap most people fall into is creating a category for every single merchant they might visit. Coffee. Fast food. Sit-down restaurants. Bars. Concert tickets. Streaming services. Movies. Books. Magazines. Games. Hobbies. Suddenly you've got twenty-three categories and you're spending more time deciding which envelope a purchase belongs in than you are actually managing your money.

That's not a budget. That's homework. And you'll quit.

So here's the test: if you can't remember which category something belongs to within two seconds of buying it, you have too many categories.

The other extreme is just as bad. I've seen people try to run their entire budget with three envelopes: bills, food, everything else. And sure, that's simple. But "everything else" becomes a dumping ground where you have no idea if you're overspending on clothes or entertainment or gas because it's all mixed together. You lose the one thing that makes envelope budgeting powerful: the ability to see exactly where your money is going.

The sweet spot, the place where this actually works, is when your categories are broad enough that you're not constantly splitting hairs, but specific enough that you can spot patterns.

Here's what that looks like in practice.

Instead of separate envelopes for coffee, fast food, and restaurants, you might have one "eating out" envelope. Instead of separate envelopes for Netflix, Spotify, and your newspaper subscription, you have "subscriptions." Instead of envelopes for shampoo, laundry detergent, and trash bags, you have "household supplies."

You're grouping by *type of spending*, not by *specific store*. And when you do that, you end up with somewhere around eight to ten categories that cover everything without drowning you in detail.

But here's where people get stuck: they want to know the *right* categories before they start. They want the perfect system handed to them, and they won't begin until they have it. That's backwards. You can't know what categories you need until you've tracked your spending for a month and seen where the money actually goes.

So start simple. Start with the bare minimum: housing, utilities, food, transportation, debt, and one catch-all called "other." That's six. Run that for a month. At the end of the month, look at "other." What's in there? If you see a pattern—let's say half of "other" is clothing purchases—then next month, pull "clothing" out and give it its own envelope. If a quarter of "other" is entertainment, pull that out too. If the rest is random one-off purchases that don't fit a pattern, leave them in "other" and move on.

You're not designing the system. You're discovering it.

And this is the part nobody tells you: your categories will change. Not every month, but over time, absolutely. When you first start budgeting, you might need a "debt" envelope because you're paying off credit cards. Six months later, the cards are paid off and that envelope disappears. You might start a "car repair" envelope after your check engine light comes on and you realize you have no plan for that. You might combine "household supplies" and "groceries" because you always buy them at the same store anyway and separating them feels pointless.

The system isn't static. It grows with you. And the categories that matter in January might be totally different from the ones that matter in June, and that's fine. That's not failure. That's learning.

But there's one category that almost everyone needs and almost nobody thinks to include at first: the "I forgot about this" envelope.

You know what I'm talking about. The annual Amazon Prime renewal. The car registration that only happens once a year. The friend's wedding in October. The vet bill for your dog's checkup. The holiday gifts. The oil change. These aren't surprises. They're predictable expenses that you forget to predict.

Most people handle these by panicking when they show up and either blowing the budget that month or putting them on a credit card. Both options feel terrible. But if you have an envelope—call it "annual expenses" or "irregular expenses" or "non-monthly bills"—and you put a little money in it every month, those expenses stop being emergencies. They're just... expected.

Here's how it works. Add up everything you spend in a year that doesn't happen monthly. Registration fees, memberships, holiday spending, back-to-school costs, whatever. Let's say it's twelve hundred dollars. Divide that by twelve. That's a hundred dollars a month. Every month, a hundred dollars goes into that envelope. Then when the bill shows up, the money's already there. You're not scrambling. You're not stressed. You planned for it.

This one category—this one simple acknowledgment that not every expense happens on a monthly cycle—will save you more stress than almost anything else in your budget.

And once you have that in place, once you've figured out your six or eight or ten categories and you've started funding them, you'll notice something shift. The budget stops feeling like a restriction and starts feeling like a map. You're not guessing anymore. You're not hoping. You know exactly what you have, what it's for, and whether you can afford the thing you're looking at. That's not control in a punishing way. That's freedom in the most practical sense of the word.

So don't overthink the categories. Start simple, track for a month, adjust. You'll know what you need when you see where the money's going. And the system you end up with won't look like anyone else's, because it's not supposed to. It's yours.

My grandmother would turn those envelopes over in her hands, feeling the worn paper.

My grandmother would turn those envelopes over in her hands, feeling the worn paper. It wasn't about deprivation; it was a physical act of intention.

Chapter 4: The Framework: The Three-Envelope Rule

90% of people who start a detailed budget abandon it within 30 days. We're not wired for constant vigilance; our brains crave simplicity and autopilot.

I know this because I've seen the spreadsheets. Hundreds of them, over the years, sent by readers asking why their budget isn't working. And they all have the same problem: forty-two categories when they need three. "Transportation" split into Gas, Car Payment, Insurance, Maintenance, Registration, Parking. "Food" subdivided into Groceries, Dining Out, Coffee Shops, Work Lunches, Snacks. "Entertainment" fractured into Streaming Services, Movies, Concerts, Books, Hobbies.

Every one of these categories represents a decision you'll have to make. Not once. Dozens of times a month. Was the coffee you grabbed at the airport "Dining Out" or "Travel"? Is the Netflix subscription "Entertainment" or "Utilities" since you consider it as essential as electricity? When you bought that book on productivity, did it go under "Personal Development" or "Books" or "Entertainment"?

These aren't meaningful financial questions. They're cognitive speed bumps that slowly exhaust you until you stop tracking altogether.

Sarah, a graphic designer in Portland, showed me her budget last year. She'd color-coded twenty-eight categories. She had tags. She had subcategories with rollover calculations. She'd spent an entire Sunday setting it up, and it was genuinely impressive—the kind of thing that would make a financial planner nod approvingly.

It lasted eleven days.

On day twelve, she bought her daughter a book at Target along with some groceries and a pack of socks. Three categories in one transaction. She meant to split it out later that evening, but her daughter had a meltdown about homework, and by the time Sarah got her to bed, the last thing she wanted to do was parse a Target receipt. She'd do it tomorrow. Except tomorrow brought its own chaos, and by the weekend, she had six transactions waiting to be categorized, and the gap between her budget and reality felt insurmountable. So she stopped. The elaborate system she'd built became another bookmark in her browser, another reminder of her supposed inability to "adult" properly.

But here's what actually failed: not Sarah. The system.

The real cost of budget complexity isn't the five minutes it takes to log an expense. It's the accumulated friction—the cognitive overhead, the decision fatigue, the growing sense that you're failing at something that shouldn't be this hard. I've watched this pattern destroy more budgets than overspending ever has.

And here's the part nobody tells you: every additional category makes your budget *worse*, not better.

More granular tracking feels like progress. It feels sophisticated, like you're finally getting serious about money. But sophistication in budgeting is usually just procrastination wearing a suit. A budget with forty-seven categories and color-coded subcategories isn't a tool. It's a second job you didn't apply for and won't get paid to do.

I know because I built one of those monsters myself.

This was maybe eight years ago, when I was convinced that the key to financial control was perfect information. I had separate line items for “Coffee at home” versus “Coffee out.” I tracked every gallon of gas with the odometer reading and price per gallon. I had a category called “Miscellaneous Personal Care Items” that I used maybe twice. I built pivot tables. I ran monthly trend analyses. I felt like a financial genius.

For six weeks.

Then I went on a long weekend trip and came back to a backlog of receipts I hadn’t entered. The gap in my data felt like a moral failure. I’d broken my perfect tracking record. And once the record was broken, what was the point? I’d have incomplete data for that month anyway. Might as well start fresh next month.

Except next month, I missed a few days and told myself the same thing. And pretty soon I wasn’t tracking anything, and the elaborate system I’d built was just another file on my desktop, judging me silently every time I saw it.

That failure taught me more than any success could have. It forced me to ask a different question: What’s the *minimum* amount of structure that would actually work?

Not the most detailed. Not the most impressive to show a financial advisor. Just the simplest system that would give me control without requiring a degree in accounting or twenty minutes a day I didn’t have.

The answer turned out to be almost embarrassingly simple.

Three envelopes. That’s it.

I know what you're thinking—three categories can't possibly capture the nuance of real financial life. What about irregular expenses that don't fit neatly? What about saving for multiple different goals? What about the seventeen different things you need to track just to feel like you know where your money's going?

That instinct, right there—that's exactly what keeps people trapped in systems they abandon within a month.

You're not aiming for perfect taxonomic accuracy. You're not building a financial museum where every purchase gets properly labeled and displayed. You're trying to make *conscious choices* about where your money goes in a way that's sustainable enough you'll still be doing it in six months when the novelty has worn off and you're just trying to get through Tuesday.

Here's the framework: Needs, Wants, and Savings.

Three envelopes. That's the whole thing.

Needs is your life-support system.

This is rent or mortgage. Utilities that keep your home livable—electricity, water, heat. Groceries, and I mean actual food, not the artisanal cheese plate and the twenty-dollar bottle of olive oil you convinced yourself was a pantry staple. Transportation that gets you to work. Basic health insurance. Essential medications. Minimum debt payments, because defaulting has consequences you can't afford.

The test for whether something belongs in Needs is brutal but clarifying: *What would happen if I didn't pay for this next month?*

If the answer involves eviction, hunger, losing your job, or a medical crisis, it's a Need. If the answer is "I'd be annoyed" or "I'd miss it" or "I'd have to make do with something less convenient," it's not a Need. It goes somewhere else.

This category shouldn't feel exciting. These are the expenses you barely think about because they're the foundation everything else rests on. They're the floor, not the furniture. And if your floor is shaky, nothing else matters.

Maria, a paralegal in Phoenix, kept insisting her $180-a-month car payment was a Need. And the *car* was, absolutely—Phoenix public transit wasn't getting her to the law office reliably, and she had a kid to drop off at school. But that specific car payment? That was a choice she'd made three years earlier when a dealership convinced her that buying new was the responsible option. She'd driven off the lot in a shiny sedan, feeling like she'd made it, and now she owed $14,000 on something worth maybe $16,000.

When her hours got cut and money got tight, she finally looked at that payment differently. The car was a Need. That particular car was a Want disguised as a Need. Six months later, she sold it, bought a $7,000 used Honda with the equity, and redirected that $180 a month toward her future instead of her past.

Wants is everything else you spend money on to make life feel worth living.

All of it. Entertainment, restaurants, coffee shops, streaming services, the gym membership you use twice a month. Hobbies. Vacations. Gifts. Clothing beyond basic replacements. The organic groceries, the nicer car, the latest phone when your current one works fine. The concert tickets. The books you could get from the library but prefer to own. The candle that smells like a bookstore even though you already have four candles you haven't burned yet.

This is consumption. Present-tense life. The money you spend on *right now* instead of later.

The line between Needs and Wants blurs sometimes, and that's fine. You don't need a philosophy degree to figure it out. A basic phone plan that keeps you connected? Probably a Need in 2026. Upgrading to the newest model every year because you like the camera? Want. A thirty-dollar-a-month bare-bones cell plan? Need. The unlimited premium plan because you stream video on your commute instead of downloading podcasts on wifi? Want.

What matters isn't achieving perfect categorization. What matters is seeing the number—really seeing how much of your income you're spending on immediate consumption versus everything else.

For most people, that number is shocking.

James, a software developer in Austin, thought he was pretty responsible with money. He maxed out his 401(k) match. He had six months of expenses in savings. He wasn't in debt. So when I suggested he try the three-envelope system, he figured it would just confirm what he already knew: that he had his act together.

Then he looked at his Wants envelope.

He was bringing home $6,800 a month after taxes and retirement contributions. His Needs were about $2,200—rent in a decent but not fancy apartment, utilities, groceries he actually cooked, car insurance, gas. That left $4,600 for Wants and Savings combined.

He was putting $500 a month into savings beyond his 401(k).

Which meant he was spending $4,100 a month on Wants.

Door Dash orders three, four times a week because he didn't feel like cooking. Bar tabs that somehow added up to $400 a month—just a couple drinks after work, nothing crazy, except it was three nights a week. A storage unit full of camping gear and photography equipment he hadn't touched in a year but kept paying $130 a month to house because someday he'd get back into those hobbies. Subscription services he'd forgotten he was paying for. Concert tickets. Weekend trips. The running joke among his friends about how James always picked up the check.

He wasn't drowning. He was making good money, and he had enough margin that $4,100 a month in Wants wasn't breaking him. But seeing it as a single number—not as individual transactions that felt reasonable in the moment, but as a category that revealed a pattern—made him angry.

Not at me. At himself. At the gap between who he thought he was and what his spending actually said about his priorities.

Anger burned off after a day or two. What remained was clarity. He didn't need to become some ascetic monk who never enjoyed anything. He just needed to *choose* his wants consciously instead of accumulating them on autopilot. He cut his Wants budget to $2,400 and bumped Savings to $2,200. The first month was awkward—he had to actually decide whether the Thursday night drinks were worth it, whether he really wanted that new lens or just liked the idea of wanting it. But by month three, he wasn't thinking about it anymore. The system had become automatic, and the Savings envelope was growing faster than it ever had.

Savings is every dollar you're setting aside for later.

Not just an emergency fund, though that's where you start. This is retirement accounts, down payment funds, car replacement savings, your kid's college fund, the vacation you're planning for next year, the medical deductible you know you'll hit eventually. Anything you're putting away for a future version of yourself to use.

Here's the psychological shift this creates: in most budgets, savings is whatever's left after you've paid your bills and spent on everything else. Which means it's usually nothing, or close enough to nothing that it feels pointless. The three-envelope system flips that. You decide how much goes to Savings based on your goals and timeline, and then Wants gets whatever remains after both Needs and Savings take their share.

Angela, a dental hygienist and single mom in Louisville, pushed back hard when I first suggested this. "I barely have enough for Wants as it is," she said. "How am I supposed to cut that even more to fund Savings?"

But when we actually looked at her numbers, she'd been spending about $900 a month on Wants and saving nothing. Not because she couldn't save. Because saving happened last, after everything else, when the money was already gone.

When she committed to putting $400 a month into Savings *first* and limiting Wants to $600, something unexpected happened. She didn't feel more deprived. She felt more in control. And watching that Savings envelope grow—$400, then $800, then $1,200, then $2,400—created a motivation she'd never felt when saving was just an aspiration with no funding behind it.

So how much should go into each envelope?

The common framework is 50-60% to Needs, 20-30% to Wants, and 10-20% to Savings, based on your after-tax income—the money that actually hits your bank account after all the withholdings.

But your life might not fit that template, and that's fine. If you're in a high-cost city and your rent alone eats 40% of your income, you might be running 70% Needs, 15% Wants, 15% Savings. If you're in a lower-cost area with a paid-off car and modest housing, maybe it's 45% Needs, 25% Wants, 30% Savings. If you're digging out from under debt, your Needs number might be higher because those minimum payments are non-negotiable.

The percentages matter less than the *intentionality*. You're not trying to hit some expert's ideal ratio. You're trying to build a system that funds your present life, your future security, and your immediate enjoyment in a way that doesn't leave you either broke or resentful.

Let me show you how this works in practice.

Angela brings home $3,800 a month after taxes. Before the three-envelope system, money felt like water running through her hands—she knew it was flowing, but she couldn't tell you where it was going.

First step: she listed her Needs. Rent: $1,250. Car payment and insurance: $380. Groceries for herself and her seven-year-old: $450. Utilities: $180. Basic phone plan: $50. Prescriptions: $40. Gas: $120.

Total Needs: $2,470.

That left $1,330 for Wants and Savings combined. And this is where the system stopped being theoretical and became uncomfortable, because Angela would have told you—had told me, in fact—that she had no money for savings. But she wasn't spending $2,470 a month. She was spending all $3,800. Which meant that extra $1,330 was going *somewhere*.

She started tracking her Wants for two weeks, not to judge herself, just to see. Streaming services: $45. Eating out and takeout: $400. Clothes and personal care: $150. Entertainment and activities for her daughter: $100. Random purchases she didn't plan for: $80. Gym membership she used maybe twice a month: $35.

Total Wants: $810 a month.

That still left $520 unaccounted for. It was leaking out in ATM withdrawals, Venmo transfers she didn't track, autopay subscriptions she'd forgotten existed. The fog she'd been living in.

She made a decision: $400 to Savings, $600 to Wants. That meant cutting Wants by $210. Gym membership canceled—$35 saved. Takeout budget capped at $250 instead of $400—$150 saved. One streaming service gone—$15 saved. Random purchases capped at $60 with a one-week waiting period before buying anything unplanned—$20 saved. That got her to $220 in reductions.

The first month felt tight. She hit her Wants limit on the 26th. Her daughter wanted to go see a movie. Angela said no, and felt like she was failing as a parent. But she didn't cheat. She didn't pull from Savings to cover it. She told her daughter they'd go next month, and they'd plan for it this time, maybe make it special.

Second month was easier. Third month, she wasn't thinking about the system anymore. It had become automatic. And the Savings envelope—$400, then $800, then $1,200—started changing how she felt about money entirely. She wasn't living paycheck to paycheck anymore. She was building something. For the first time in years, she felt like she was getting ahead instead of just keeping up.

You might be wondering: what about irregular expenses? The car registration that comes once a year, the insurance premium that hits every six months, the back-to-school shopping, the holiday gifts everyone expects?

They go in Savings—at least functionally. You're setting aside money now for something you'll spend later. Some people create a fourth envelope called "Irregular" to keep it separate. Others track it as a subcategory within Savings. The mechanism matters less than the principle: if you *know* an expense is coming, you save for it in small monthly chunks instead of getting blindsided when it arrives.

Angela knew her car registration was $280, due in September. Starting in January, she added $25 a month to a "car registration" fund within her Savings envelope. By September, she had $200 set aside. The remaining $80 came from that month's cash flow without derailing everything. Same with holiday gifts—$50 a month starting in January gave her $600 by December, money she could spend guilt-free because she'd planned for it.

This still sounds like work though, doesn't it? Tracking subcategories, planning for irregular expenses, allocating money across envelopes?

Here's the thing: you're not tracking *transactions*. You're tracking *envelopes*.

When Angela buys groceries, she doesn't log "groceries, $73.42, Needs category, food subcategory, Kroger, March 14th." She just knows it comes from Needs, and once or twice a week she glances at her bank balance and knows roughly how much is left in that envelope. The categories are big enough that individual purchases don't require thought. You're not making forty micro-decisions a month. You're making three big ones: Needs, Wants, Savings.

And if even that feels like too much tracking—if you're the kind of person who knows you won't log into a budgeting app more than once—you can make it automatic.

Set up your bank account so that when your paycheck hits, money moves automatically. A fixed amount transfers immediately to a separate savings account—your Savings envelope. Another fixed amount goes to a bills-only checking account that handles Needs on autopay. Whatever's left stays in your main checking account—your Wants envelope.

Now you're not tracking anything. The system is structural.

Michael, a high school history teacher in Cleveland, set this up when he realized he'd never stick with manual tracking. His paycheck was $4,200 a month after taxes. On payday, $900 auto-transferred to a savings account at a different bank. Another $2,500 went to a bills-only checking account with autopay set up for rent, utilities, car payment, insurance, student loan. The remaining $800 stayed in his main checking account. That was his Wants money. He didn't track it. He didn't budget it. He just spent it, knowing that when it was gone, he was done until next payday.

Some months he'd run out by the 25th and coast on leftovers and Netflix for a few days. Other months he'd have $100 left over and move it to savings as a bonus. The system required zero ongoing effort beyond the twenty minutes it took to set up the automatic transfers.

Could he have optimized further? Probably. Could he have tracked his Wants spending more carefully and found efficiencies? Sure. But he *wasn't going to do that*, and he knew it. The system he built wasn't perfect. It was sustainable. And sustainability beats perfection every single time, because a perfect system you abandon in three weeks is worth nothing, while a simple system you actually use for years is worth everything.

That's the real insight of the three-envelope framework. It's not the *most accurate* way to budget. It's not the most detailed or sophisticated. It's not going to win awards from financial planners who love spreadsheets.

It's just the one you'll actually still be using six months from now when the novelty wears off, when life gets chaotic, when you're tired and stressed and the last thing you want to do is categorize seventeen purchases from a weekend grocery run.

The system works not because it's perfect, but because it's simple enough to survive contact with your real life.

So here's what I want you to do, right now, before you move on to the next chapter: take out a piece of paper or open a notes app, and write down your after-tax monthly income at the top. Then make three lines: Needs, Wants, Savings. Don't overthink it. Just estimate—what do you think you're spending in each bucket right now? Write those numbers down.

Look at them.

Are they honest? Is your Wants number higher than you want to admit? Is your Savings number zero, or close to it?

Good. That's your starting point. Not where you wish you were. Where you actually are.

Because the Miller family—the real worked example you're about to see in the next chapter—started exactly where you are right now. Three envelopes, a bunch of expenses that didn't fit neatly, and no idea whether this would actually work in real life.

That forty-second category list feels less like empowerment and more like a self-imposed prison – each item demanding our attention while the larger financial picture remains obscured.

Chapter 5: Worked Example: The Miller Family

Sarah Miller sat at her kitchen table on a Tuesday morning in March, staring at a credit card statement. The number at the bottom—$4,347.82—wasn't catastrophic. They weren't drowning. But she couldn't remember what half of it was for.

That's the part that got to her. Not the amount itself—they'd had higher balances before, they'd managed. It was the *blankness* of it. Like trying to remember what you ate for lunch four days ago. The money had left. Where did it go?

Sarah teaches fifth grade. Her husband David does IT support for a healthcare system. Combined, they make about $85,000 a year—comfortable by most measures, enough to own a modest three-bedroom house in a decent school district, enough to keep one car payment current alongside the mortgage. They're not living paycheck to paycheck in the dramatic sense you see in headlines, the kind where people choose between groceries and electricity. They're living in that murkier middle ground where the money *should* work, where they *should* have margin, but somehow it never quite materializes.

Two weeks before that Tuesday morning, their Honda CRV had needed a brake job. Not optional. Not luxury. The kind of repair that happens when you own a seven-year-old car with 90,000 miles on it and you hear a grinding noise that the guy at the mechanic's shop describes with the phrase "you really don't want to wait on this." The estimate was $680.

They didn't have $680 sitting around.

They had maybe $200 in what they optimistically called their "emergency fund," which was really just the checking account balance that hadn't been spoken for yet. So the brake job went on the credit card. And then, because the brake job had maxed out the emotional bandwidth for financial stress that week, they didn't look at the credit card statement when it arrived. Sarah stuck it on the counter under a stack of mail. It sat there for ten days before she opened it.

Now she was looking at $4,347.82 and doing that mental archaeology—trying to reconstruct what purchases had built this number. The brake job, obviously. Groceries, probably a thousand dollars over the past month, maybe more. Gas. The vet visit when their cat had been limping. The school fundraiser where she'd bought wrapping paper she didn't need because it felt awkward to say no to a colleague's kid. The Target run that was supposed to be "just toiletries" but somehow ended up at $130. That dinner out two Saturdays ago when neither of them felt like cooking and they'd ordered Thai food and it was $65 with tip.

None of it extravagant. All of it ordinary. And that was somehow worse.

I've seen this pattern so many times I could script it. People who make decent money, who aren't buying boats or designer handbags, who genuinely believe they're being reasonable with their spending—and they *are* being reasonable, in the moment, transaction by transaction. But reasonable spending without a *structure* is just a slow leak. You don't notice it until you're standing in a puddle.

Sarah brought the statement to David that night. He was on the couch watching something on his laptop—a YouTube video about troubleshooting network issues, which is what he does when he's decompressing. She sat down next to him and said, “We need to talk about money.”

David paused the video. That flat, careful pause that means a conversation is about to happen that neither person wants to have.

“How bad?” he asked.

“It’s not *bad* bad,” Sarah said. “We’re not in crisis. But we’re at forty-three hundred on the Visa and I don’t know how we got here.”

They’d had this conversation before. Different numbers, same shape. And it always ended the same way: they’d agree to “be more careful,” they’d halfheartedly track spending for a week or two, and then life would get busy and they’d slip back into whatever pattern had created the problem in the first place.

David makes good money. Sarah makes good money. They should not feel broke. But they did. That persistent, low-grade anxiety that showed up around the twentieth of every month, when Sarah would check their checking account balance and do mental math about what bills were still coming. The sense that they were always one unexpected expense away from chaos.

Here’s what nobody tells you about financial stress when you’re in that middle-income zone: it doesn’t feel like poverty. It feels like *failure*. Because you look around and see people who make less than you do and seem fine, and you think: what are we doing wrong?

Sarah had tried fixing this before. She’d read articles. She’d downloaded budgeting apps—three different ones over the past two years. She’d even attempted a spreadsheet once, color-coded and everything, with categories for groceries and utilities and entertainment and a catch-all “miscellaneous” that became a dumping ground for everything she didn't want to think about.

The spreadsheet lasted three weeks.

Not because Sarah lacks discipline—she's a fifth-grade teacher, she manages thirty ten-year-olds every day, she can handle complex systems. It lasted three weeks because updating a spreadsheet is one more task on a list that already includes grading papers and meal planning and remembering to sign the permission slip for the field trip and texting back her mom and keeping the house from descending into chaos.

Every budgeting system assumes you have unlimited attention. That you'll remember to log every transaction, reconcile every account, review every category. But attention is the scarcest resource in your life. More scarce than money, honestly. And any system that demands significant attention every single day is a system that will fail the moment life gets busy.

Which is every moment.

Two weeks after the credit card conversation, Sarah's sister mentioned something at a family dinner. Her sister—I'll call her Emily, though that's not her real name—is deeply into personal finance blogs and has opinions about index funds and will tell you unprompted about the difference between traditional and Roth IRAs. Normally Sarah tunes this out because Emily can be a bit much. But this time Emily said something that stuck.

"I've been doing this thing with envelopes. It sounds old-fashioned but it's actually kind of working."

Sarah asked what she meant. Emily described a system where she withdrew cash at the beginning of the month, divided it into physical envelopes by category, and that was it. When the envelope was empty, she stopped spending in that category. No app. No spreadsheet. Just cash and envelopes and the very simple feedback loop of *you can see how much is left*.

Sarah's first reaction was skepticism. Cash felt antiquated. Envelopes felt like something her grandmother might have done during the Depression, back when people buried money in coffee cans in the backyard.

But Emily had this way of talking about money that Sarah envied—calm, unbothered, like it was just another household task she'd figured out, the same tone she'd use to describe a good vacuum cleaner. Not stressed. Not anxious. Not doing mental math in the Target parking lot about whether she could afford the thing in her cart.

Sarah wanted that.

She brought it up to David that night. He was skeptical too. David's skepticism usually manifests as silence, a thoughtful pause that can mean either "I'm considering this" or "I think this is a terrible idea but don't want to say so directly." In this case, it was the former.

"So we'd just... use cash for everything?" he asked.

"I think just for some things. The stuff that varies. I don't know, I'm just tired of feeling like this."

David was quiet for a moment. Then: "Yeah. Me too."

They decided to try it for one month. Not a forever commitment. Not some grand overhaul of their entire financial life. Just one month, three envelopes, see what happens.

The framework they'd read about—the Three-Envelope Rule—breaks spending into Needs, Wants, and Savings. That's it. Not seventeen subcategories. Not separate line items for groceries vs. household supplies vs. personal care. Just three big buckets.

Here's what that looked like in real numbers for the Millers:

They bring home $4,000 a month after taxes and health insurance and 401k contributions. Not their gross income—nobody budgets on gross income, that's delusional, you can't spend money the government already took—but the actual amount that hits their checking account twice a month. Four thousand dollars. That's what they had to work with.

First step: the Look Back.

Sarah sat down with their bank statements from February and started categorizing. Not perfectly. Not with forensic precision. Just a rough sense of where the money had actually gone. She made a list on a legal pad—I've seen it, she showed it to me later, and her handwriting is the kind of scratchy half-cursive that teachers develop from years of writing fast comments on student work.

Mortgage: $1,450. That's fixed, non-negotiable.

Car payment: $320. Same.

Utilities averaged around $180. Could vary slightly month to month—higher in summer with AC, higher in winter with heat—but call it $180.

Car insurance: $140. Phone bill: $95. Internet: $60.

These were the non-negotiables. The things that didn't care whether they felt like paying them or not.

Running total: $2,245.

Then came the messier category. Groceries—she scrolled through their bank statement and added up every trip to the grocery store, every Target run that included food, every convenience store stop for milk. About $850 for the month. More than she'd expected.

Gas: $200. Again, more than she'd guessed. David's commute was twenty-five minutes each way. She drove less but still had to get to school and back.

Then the miscellaneous stuff that doesn't fit clean categories but still costs money: the vet bill, the school fundraiser, the Girl Scout cookies they bought from a neighbor's kid to be polite, the replacement water bottle their daughter needed when she lost hers, the birthday present for a classmate's party, the co-pay for Sarah's dentist appointment, the air filter for the furnace, the pack of lightbulbs, the bottle of Advil, the—

She stopped itemizing and just added it all up. About $750 for the month in this catch-all category of "things that came up."

Her running total was now $4,045.

But they'd only brought home $4,000.

Which meant either she'd miscategorized something or they'd been spending forty-five dollars more than they made every month, floating it on the credit card. Given the credit card balance, she suspected the latter.

Actually, it was probably worse than that. Because she hadn't included the brake job in this calculation—that was an anomaly, a one-time thing. But there was always a one-time thing. Last month it had been new tires. The month before that, their daughter had needed glasses. Before that, the washing machine had made a noise and they'd called a repair guy who charged $150 to replace a belt.

This is the part where most budgeting advice tells you to cut everything. Cancel subscriptions. Make coffee at home. Adopt a scarcity mindset. Stop buying luxuries.

But here's the thing: the Millers weren't buying luxuries. They didn't have subscriptions to cancel—no Netflix, no Spotify premium, no meal kit delivery. Sarah made coffee at home already. David's idea of a splurge was a $3.50 coffee from the local place twice a week, and even that he felt vaguely guilty about.

What they needed wasn't a lecture on deprivation. They needed a system that acknowledged reality: they were going to spend money on groceries and gas and vet bills and school fundraisers because that's what living a normal human life requires. The question wasn't *whether* to spend money on those things. The question was *how much* and *how to keep it from bleeding into chaos*.

So they set up three envelopes.

Envelope one: Needs. This got $2,500.

That covered the fixed bills—mortgage, car payment, utilities, insurance, phone, internet—plus a realistic grocery budget ($900, slightly higher than February's average because she wanted some buffer), plus gas ($200), plus a cushion for the household expenses that show up without warning. Lightbulbs. Toilet paper. The stuff that doesn't feel like shopping but somehow costs money.

Envelope two: Wants. They allocated $1,000 here.

You might be thinking: a thousand dollars for *wants*? Isn't that excessive?

And look, I get it. A thousand dollars sounds like a lot for discretionary spending. But here's what was in that category: David's coffee habit. Sarah's monthly nail appointment—the one thing she does for herself that isn't groceries or laundry or cleaning up after other people. Eating out, not fancy restaurants but the pizza place on Friday when neither of them felt like cooking. The occasional movie. A birthday present for a family member. New shoes for their daughter when she outgrows the old ones. The streaming service they share with Sarah's parents. The Girl Scout cookies. The Target run for "just a few things" that ends up being sixty bucks.

They're not monks. The goal wasn't to eliminate joy from their lives. It was to make it *conscious*. To put a boundary around it so it didn't expand to fill every available dollar.

Envelope three: Savings. This got $500.

Which, if you're doing math, adds up to $4,000. No surplus. No cushion. Just a plan to stop the bleeding and start directing their money with intention.

David went to the bank on a Friday afternoon and asked for four thousand dollars in various bills. The teller—a woman in her fifties with reading glasses on a chain—asked if everything was okay.

"Yeah," David said. "Just trying something new with the budget."

She gave him a look that was either polite concern or mild confusion. He felt vaguely embarrassed, like he was explaining a hobby she wouldn't understand.

He came home with a bank envelope full of cash. They used actual manila envelopes from the office supply store—the kind with the little metal clasp. Sarah labeled them in her teacher handwriting: NEEDS, WANTS, SAVINGS.

They divided the cash. It sat on the kitchen counter in a small stack, and for the first time in months, maybe years, they could *see* their money.

Not as a digital number on a screen that fluctuated based on what had cleared and what hadn't, not as an abstract concept they'd spend and replenish in some vague cycle. But as a physical thing. Finite. Real.

That visibility changed everything.

The first week was awkward.

Sarah went to the grocery store on Sunday—her usual routine—and brought the Needs envelope. She'd estimated $150 for the week's groceries. Standard shopping trip: milk, bread, eggs, chicken, some vegetables, pasta, cereal for their daughter, snacks, the basics.

Halfway through the store, she glanced in her cart and did the math. She was already at $130 and hadn't hit the meat section yet.

She paused. Looked at the cart. Started making decisions.

Put back the fancy crackers—the organic ones with the seeds that cost $5.99 instead of the regular ones at $2.49. Swapped the name-brand cereal for store brand. Picked the family pack of chicken thighs instead of the individually wrapped breasts because it was three dollars cheaper per pound and she could portion it herself.

Not because they couldn't afford those things in the abstract. They could. If she'd put them on the debit card, the transaction would have gone through fine. But the envelope only had $150, and she was staring at the physical reality of that limit.

She spent $148.

Left the store feeling vaguely accomplished in a way that surprised her. It wasn't about the two dollars she'd saved. It was about the *awareness*. For years—maybe her entire adult life—she'd grocery shopped with a vague sense of trying not to overspend, but what did that even mean when it all went on a card and she didn't see the impact until later, if ever?

Now she'd made a dozen small decisions—brand swaps, putting back the impulse buys near the checkout, choosing the cheaper cut of meat—that added up to staying within a boundary she'd set for herself. And it didn't feel like deprivation. It felt like *steering*.

David had a harder time with it.

His coffee habit wasn't dramatic—he's not a five-dollar-latte guy. But he did stop at a local place most mornings on the way to work. Three-fifty for a medium coffee. Familiar routine. The barista knew his order. It was a small moment of normalcy before he walked into an office where people expected him to fix their computer problems all day.

The first Monday with the envelope system, he pulled money from the Wants envelope for his coffee. Handed over the cash. Got his change. The transaction took maybe fifteen seconds longer than swiping a card.

But it felt different.

Not morally different. Not like he was doing something wrong. Just... different. The transaction had *weight*. He could see the money leaving his hand. Could see the Wants envelope getting a little lighter.

By Wednesday, he'd started making coffee at home twice a week.

Not because Sarah gave him a hard time about it. She didn't. Not because he felt guilty. But because he looked at the Wants envelope on Wednesday morning and realized he wanted to spend some of that money on other things—maybe the new video game he'd been eyeing, maybe dinner out with Sarah on their anniversary next month—and the coffee felt less important in that context.

This is the shift that happens when you move from invisible spending to visible spending. It's not about guilt or restriction. It's about *trade-offs*. You can't see a trade-off when money is an abstraction. But when it's sitting in an envelope on your counter, the trade-off is right there in front of you.

You might be wondering: isn't this just deprivation with extra steps? Isn't cash-stuffing just a more inconvenient way to feel restricted?

I'll be honest with you—it can feel that way at first. Especially if you're coming from a place where spending has been mostly unconscious. That first moment when you want something and you look in the envelope and realize you need to make a choice, that can feel like being told no.

But here's the shift the Millers experienced—and that I've seen happen with almost everyone who sticks with this system past the first uncomfortable month:

Restriction feels like someone else telling you no.

Boundaries feel like *you* telling yourself yes to the things that matter.

When Sarah decided not to buy the fancy crackers, she wasn't being punished by the budget. She was honoring a decision she'd already made—that $150 was the right amount to spend on groceries that week—so she could spend the Wants money on something she valued more. That's not deprivation. That's agency.

There's a particular kind of anxiety that comes from invisible money. I'm not sure we have a good word for it in English. It's that feeling when you're about to buy something—standing in line at Target, cart full of stuff you need (or think you need, or might need)—and you're doing mental math about whether you can afford it. Not whether the transaction will go through. It probably will. But whether you *should* be spending this money right now given everything else that's coming up this month.

That anxiety disappeared for the Millers by week two.

Not because they suddenly had more money. They didn't. But because the question "can I afford this?" had a concrete answer. Look in the envelope. Either the money's there or it isn't.

No mental math. No checking the account balance on your phone in the parking lot. No wondering if this purchase is going to be the one that tips you into overdraft or makes you short on the electric bill next week.

Just: look in the envelope.

By the end of month one, they'd overspent Needs by about $80. Turns out their grocery estimate was low—$900 sounded reasonable but they were actually spending closer to $950-$1000 when you included all the random household stuff that shows up at the grocery store. Paper towels. Dish soap. The poster board their daughter needed for a school project that Sarah picked up while getting milk.

They'd underspent Wants by $120. Partly because of David's coffee adjustment. Partly because they just became more conscious about small purchases. The impulse buys at checkout. The "let's just order in" nights that happened less often when they had to pull cash from the envelope and watch it go.

The Savings envelope sat untouched. Five hundred dollars they hadn't spent, hadn't borrowed from, hadn't raided for an emergency.

That felt like a miracle.

Not a big miracle. Not the kind of financial transformation you read about in clickbait articles where someone pays off six figures of debt in a year. Just the quiet miracle of making it through a month without going backward.

Month two, they adjusted.

This is important: the system isn't static. You're not locked into the first numbers you pick. Sarah moved $80 from Wants to Needs to better reflect their actual grocery spending. They also got more specific within the Wants category—not separate envelopes, just a mental note about what that money was for.

David's coffee and occasional lunch out: maybe $150 for the month.

Sarah's nail appointment: $40.

Eating out as a family: $200.

Random kid stuff—birthday parties, school activities, the occasional treat: $100.

Miscellaneous actual wants—a new book, a video game, whatever came up: the rest.

They didn't track these subcategories obsessively. It was just a loose framework to keep the Wants envelope from becoming a free-for-all.

They also started having a weekly money date. Saturday morning, coffee at the kitchen table, ten minutes to check the envelopes and see where they stood.

These weren't fights. They weren't tense. They were just... updates.

"Looks like we're running low on Needs, probably need to be careful with groceries this week."

"I'm thinking about using some of the Wants money for that concert ticket—sound good?"

"Yeah, go for it. I already got my thing this month."

Simple. Undramatic. Collaborative.

Before the envelopes, money conversations happened in one of two modes: crisis (when a bill was overdue or an unexpected expense hit) or avoidance (the rest of the time). The crisis conversations were stressful. The avoidance was worse—this low-level tension that lived in the background of their relationship, never quite addressed, always simmering.

Now they talked about money the way they talked about anything else. What's for dinner. Who's picking up the kid from soccer. How much is left in the Wants envelope.

The Savings envelope became something different than it had been in their previous attempts. Before, "savings" had been an abstraction. Money they *intended* to set aside but usually didn't because something always came up. It existed as a concept, a thing they believed in theoretically, like flossing or drinking eight glasses of water a day.

Now it was physical. They could see it growing.

By the end of month two, they had a thousand dollars in that envelope. By month three, fifteen hundred.

Sarah moved it to a savings account at that point because storing that much cash at home made her nervous—she kept imagining their house catching fire or someone breaking in, and fifteen hundred dollars going up in smoke or walking out the door felt like a risk not worth taking.

But she kept the envelope. It sat there labeled SAVINGS, and every month they'd put five hundred in it, and then once it got to a certain amount—say a thousand—she'd deposit it at the bank and write the new total on the envelope in pencil.

They decided to use part of that money for something specific: knocking down the credit card balance.

That number that had been sitting at $4,347.82 when Sarah first stared at the statement in March? They paid it down to $3,200 in April. Then $2,800 in May. Then $2,300 in June.

Not because they'd suddenly gotten a raise. Not because they'd won the lottery or gotten a tax refund. But because they'd stopped unconsciously adding to it every month and started directing money toward it with intention.

Here's what surprised them most, and what Sarah told me when we talked about this several months in: they didn't feel deprived.

If anything, they felt more freedom.

Because when you know exactly what you have and what it's for, you stop carrying around that low-grade anxiety about whether you can afford something. The answer is right there in the envelope. Either the money's there or it isn't. And if it's not, that's not a moral failing. It's just information. You wait, or you adjust, or you make a different choice.

I remember Sarah saying, "It's like the envelopes gave me permission to spend money on things I enjoy without feeling guilty. Because I knew I'd already accounted for it. The money was there *for that*."

That's the thing about boundaries. We think of them as restrictive. But good boundaries are actually freeing. They tell you where the edges are so you can move around inside them without constantly second-guessing yourself.

Month four, their cat got sick.

I mentioned the cat earlier—older, kind of cranky, the type of cat that tolerates the family but doesn't particularly like any of them. He stopped eating. Started hiding under the bed. Sarah took him to the vet.

The vet bill was $380. Blood work, X-rays, medication. Not optional. Not negotiable. The cat needed medical care.

They didn't have a "pet emergency" envelope. That hadn't occurred to them when they set up the system.

Sarah looked at David. David looked at Sarah. They pulled from Savings.

It felt like a setback. They'd been making progress on the credit card. They'd built up a cushion. And now they were spending it on the cat.

But here's the thing: they *covered* the vet bill without panic. Without scrambling. Without that sinking feeling of "how are we going to pay for this" or "I guess it's going on the credit card."

The envelope system had given them enough buffer to handle a surprise without it derailing everything. The cat got better. The Savings envelope went down to $720. The next month they put another $500 in and climbed back over $1,200.

That's what savings is actually for. Not some distant future emergency. The emergencies that show up *now*.

They also started noticing patterns.

Turns out, they were spending about $200 a month on eating out. Not fancy restaurants—they'd been to maybe two sit-down restaurants in the past year. But the accumulated cost of "I don't feel like cooking tonight" and picking up pizza or Chinese food or driving through somewhere on the way home from work.

Once they saw that number clearly—because they were pulling cash from the Wants envelope and watching it disappear into takeout containers—they made a conscious choice: cut it to $100 and redirect the other hundred toward savings.

Not because takeout is morally wrong. Not because they were trying to win some game of financial purity. But because they valued the long-term security more than the short-term convenience. That was *their* trade-off. Someone else might make a different choice. That's fine. The point is they were *making* a choice instead of just letting it happen.

This is the part where most budget stories would tell you about the Millers' dramatic transformation. How they paid off all their debt in six months and bought a house in cash and retired early and now travel the world on passive income.

That's not this story.

The Millers are still working regular jobs. Sarah's still teaching fifth grade. David's still doing IT support. They still have a mortgage and a car payment. They still spend money on things that aren't strictly necessary because they're human beings living in the world, not characters in a financial fable.

But here's what changed:

The anxiety lifted.

That persistent feeling of being one expense away from disaster? Gone. Not because disaster can't happen. It can. But because they have a system that can absorb it.

The fighting about money? Mostly gone. Replaced by boring, undramatic conversations about envelopes and trade-offs and what they wanted to prioritize this month.

The guilt about small indulgences? Gone. Because if the money's in the envelope, it's *for* spending. That's the whole point.

Sarah told me—and this stuck with me—that the best part wasn't even the money itself. It was the *mental space*. She wasn't spending emotional energy worrying about whether they could afford something or tracking purchases in her head or feeling guilty about small indulgences. The system handled it. The envelopes held the boundaries. She could just live her life.

That's the real promise of this approach, and it's not the one most budgeting advice leads with. It's not about becoming a different person or developing iron willpower or never spending money on anything fun. It's about building a system that works *for* your brain instead of against it. A system that acknowledges you're busy and tired and human and probably not going to track every penny in a spreadsheet because who has time for that.

Now, I can already hear the objection forming in your head: this is all well and good for the Millers, but what about people who don't have $4,000 a month? What about single parents working two jobs? People with irregular income? Folks who are genuinely living paycheck to paycheck, not the comfortable middle-class version?

Fair question. And I'm not going to stand here and tell you that envelopes are some magic solution to poverty. They're not. If your income genuinely doesn't cover your expenses, no budgeting system is going to fix that. You need more money, full stop.

But the envelopes scale.

The principle—dividing your money into clear categories and making it visible—works whether you're working with four thousand dollars or fourteen hundred. The amounts change. The percentages might shift. But the core mechanism stays the same.

Let's say you're bringing home $2,000 a month. Your Needs envelope is going to be proportionally larger—maybe $1,400 or $1,500 because housing and food and transportation are less flexible when you're working with less margin. Your Wants might be $300. Your Savings might start at $50, which feels impossibly small but is infinitely more than zero.

The point isn't the amount. The point is the habit. The visibility. The practice of telling your money where to go instead of wondering where it went.

I've worked with people at all income levels—from folks making six figures who still felt broke to people scraping by on minimum wage trying to keep the lights on. The ones who succeed with this system aren't the ones with the most money. They're the ones who commit to the visibility. Who look at the envelope every time. Who make the conscious trade-offs even when it's uncomfortable.

The Millers started in May. By September—four months in—they had $3,000 in actual savings. Not money they intended to save someday. Not a vague aspiration. Money sitting in an account, earning interest (not much interest, but some), available for actual emergencies.

They'd paid the credit card down to $1,800. They'd stopped the monthly cycle of overspending without meaning to.

More than that, they'd stopped feeling like money was something that *happened* to them. It became something they directed. Not perfectly. Not without setbacks. But with enough intention that the trajectory changed.

And here's the thing nobody tells you about budgeting: the first month is the hardest, but not because of the restrictions. It's hard because you're confronting reality. You're seeing where your money actually goes, which is often different from where you think it goes or where you wish it went.

The Millers discovered they'd been spending $150 a month at Target on stuff they couldn't even remember buying. That's not a moral failure. That's just what happens when spending is frictionless and unconscious. You wander in for shampoo and walk out with shampoo plus a decorative candle plus a throw pillow plus a bag of candy plus a clearance item you didn't need but it was 70% off plus—

The envelope system adds friction back in. Not to punish you, but to wake you up. To turn spending from an autopilot behavior into a conscious choice.

And once you're awake—once you can see the shape of your money and the patterns of your spending—you can start steering.

Month six, they did something they hadn't done in years: they started talking about goals.

Not vague someday goals like "we should take a vacation" or "we should save for retirement." Specific, dated goals with price tags attached.

They wanted to take their daughter to Disney World in eighteen months. Sarah had been promising this trip for two years, always pushing it off because they couldn't afford it. Now they sat down and did the math. A modest trip—drive down instead of fly, stay off-property, pack lunches, keep it simple—would cost about $3,500.

They opened a fourth envelope. Labeled it VACATION. Started putting $200 a month into it.

That meant pulling back slightly on the aggressive credit card payments, which was a trade-off they discussed and decided was worth it. They could pay off the credit card over twelve months instead of nine and still take the vacation. The interest would cost them maybe an extra $150 total. That felt like a worthwhile trade for being able to do something as a family, make a memory, keep a promise.

You see what's happening here? They'd moved past survival mode. Past just trying not to go backward. They were planning. Making choices about what mattered to them. Building a life, not just managing crises.

That's where the envelope system takes you if you stick with it. Not to some fantasy land where money stops being a constraint. But to a place where you're in conversation with your money instead of at war with it. Where you can see what you have, decide what matters, and make it happen—not someday, but on a timeline you control.

And that shift—from chaos to clarity, from anxiety to agency—that's the worked example. Not perfect budgets or zero debt or some dramatic Before and After. Just real people figuring out a system that fits their actual life, and finding out that clarity is worth more than you'd think.

Sarah stared at the statement, not angry, but profoundly *sad*. That blankness wasn't just about money; it was about time, energy, and lost opportunities.

Sarah stared at the statement, not angry, but profoundly *sad*. That blankness wasn't just about money; it was about time, energy, and lost opportunities.

Chapter 6: Dealing with Variable Expenses

I once overdrew my checking account by $180 while I had over $2,000 sitting in savings.

The repair shop in Bellevue had just quoted me $340 for a timing belt replacement. Not catastrophic money, but enough that I needed to move it from somewhere. I pulled out my phone in their waiting room and opened my budget spreadsheet.

I might as well have been reading cuneiform.

Fixed expenses lived in checking. Variable expenses had their own bucket. The emergency fund was reserved for "major emergencies only"—a rule I'd written during a moment of financial seriousness that now felt like pure self-sabotage. There was something about not touching certain categories before the 15th. Or was it after the 15th? I couldn't remember. The mechanic was standing at the counter with my keys.

I guessed. Pulled from checking—the account I'd already drained paying the mortgage and electric bill three days earlier.

Wrong.

By the time I got home and untangled my own system, the overdraft fee sat there like a small monument to overthinking. The $2,000 in savings might as well have been in a vault in Switzerland.

That fee—$35, which the bank later stacked with a second one when a gas station charge cleared the next morning—cost me less than the mental real estate I'd wasted. I'd spent six weeks building that budget spreadsheet. Color-coded it. Added conditional formatting. The thing could practically file my taxes. But when a real expense showed up on a Tuesday afternoon, the system I'd built to protect my money had blocked me from accessing it.

Here's what nobody tells you about variable expenses: they don't become predictable just because you made a category for them.

Your transmission doesn't consult your spreadsheet before it fails. Your daughter's glasses don't wait until you've finished your monthly budget meeting with yourself before she sits on them. Medical copays arrive on a Tuesday in March. Vet emergencies happen on Saturdays. The HOA sends a special assessment letter two days before your paycheck hits, and if your system requires ten minutes of squinting at your phone to figure out which account to pull from, you don't have a budget.

You have an obstacle course where you're the only competitor.

Most budgets collapse right here. Not because people are careless—because the traditional approach insists you treat variable expenses like they're predictable when they are fundamentally, irreducibly not. The orthodoxy says: track everything, categorize everything, reconcile at month-end. Create a sinking fund for car maintenance. A separate line item for medical. Another for home repair. Build twelve sub-accounts in your head and maintain a running tally of what's where.

It's financial advice designed by people who've never stood in a transmission shop parking lot with a crying toddler in the backseat.

The writer Anne Lamott talks about her students trying to write perfect first drafts—every sentence polished, every scene complete. It paralyzes them. They produce nothing because the gap between perfect and done is too wide to cross. Budgeting has the same problem, except the stakes aren't a blank page. It's whether you overdraw your account buying groceries.

I know what you're thinking: *Isn't that what an emergency fund is for?*

Yes. But if your emergency fund has rules and subcategories and complicated if-then logic about what qualifies, you've built a different version of the same trap. I've seen people with $5,000 in savings refuse to pull $200 for a dental crown because they weren't sure if it met their own definition of "emergency." They put it on a credit card instead—16.9% APR—because the credit card didn't ask questions.

The point isn't to create a more sophisticated system. It's to create one that works when you're standing in a mechanic's waiting room with fifteen seconds to decide.

Variable expenses need space to move.

Here's the framework: stop trying to predict them. You can't schedule the windshield crack, but you can admit that rocks exist and highways are full of them. You might not know when your water heater will die, but you know it will die. The question isn't whether these expenses will hit. It's whether your system bends or breaks when they do.

In the three-envelope model from Chapter 4, variable expenses live in the same place as everything else that isn't fixed and predictable: the Spending envelope. That's it. One bucket. No subcategories. No decision tree about whether a $120 urgent care visit qualifies as "medical emergency" or "routine health." The money is there, or it isn't. If it's there, you spend it. If it isn't, you know immediately, and you make a different choice.

The elegance isn't in tracking. It's in not having to track.

When the HVAC dies in July—and it will, because HVAC systems have a perverse instinct for dying during heat waves—you don't open a spreadsheet. You look at one number. Your Spending envelope. If it can absorb the hit, you call the repair company. If it can't, you know in five seconds, and you make a different decision. Maybe you pull from savings. Maybe you put it on a card and shift next month's spending to pay it off. Maybe you get three quotes instead of one.

But you're not stuck in analysis paralysis while the house hits 89 degrees.

This is the piece most budget advice misses: variability isn't the enemy. Complexity is. Every subcategory you create, every rule you write about what qualifies and what doesn't, every conditional you build into your system—each one is a small tax on your ability to make a decision under pressure. And variable expenses only show up under pressure. That's what makes them variable.

The mechanic in Bellevue got paid, eventually. My checking account recovered. But I kept thinking about the feeling of standing in that waiting room, phone in hand, unable to access money I actually had because the system was too complex to use when it mattered.

The question kept circling back: what if you never had to open your phone at all?

That question led to something stupidly simple. I stopped trying to predict variable expenses and started reserving space for them instead.

Here's the shift: most budgeting advice treats variable expenses like a forecasting problem. You're supposed to estimate what you'll spend, then track whether you were right. The tracking becomes the work. The spreadsheet becomes the system. And when the estimate is wrong—which it always is, because that's what *variable* means—you're stuck either ignoring the system or rewriting it.

I did neither. I just started pulling a fixed amount into a separate account every month and calling it the variable fund. Not because I knew I'd spend exactly that much. Because I knew I'd spend *something*, and I wanted it handled before the question even came up.

The first month I pulled $800. It felt arbitrary. It probably was. But when the next unplannable thing hit—dog needed a vet visit, $340—I didn't open an app. I didn't check a category. I just paid it, because the money was already there, already separated, already reserved for exactly this kind of moment.

No decision fatigue. No guilt. No math.

Just: is this variable? Yes. Does the fund cover it? Yes. Done.

I realized then that spreadsheets weren't about preventing overspending. They were a record of it, presented after the fact with a side of self-recrimination.

Chapter 7: The Card System: Making it Automatic

I'm watching Jennifer sit at her kitchen table at 10:47 PM on a Tuesday, and she's close to tears. Not because anything terrible happened—her kids are asleep upstairs, her husband's watching TV in the next room, everything's fine—but because she's been trying to reconcile her credit card statement for the past ninety minutes and she still can't figure out where that extra $340 went.

That's why automating this process is so crucial. It isn't just about saving a few minutes each month. It's about reclaiming those lost moments—the ones stolen by the constant mental tax of wondering where your money went.

She's got a highlighter in one hand, the printed statement in front of her, and her phone pulled up to her bank app. Matching charges. Cross-referencing dates. Trying to remember if that $47.82 at Target was the one where she bought the birthday present or the one where she grabbed dish soap and paper towels and somehow ended up with a cart full of things she didn't plan to buy.

The statement says "TARGET" seventeen times this month.

Which one was which?

This is what the old way costs you. Not money—though Jennifer probably did overspend. It costs something more expensive: your Tuesday night. Your peace of mind. The feeling that you're in control of anything at all.

Jennifer is doing everything the traditional budgeting advice tells her to do. She's reviewing her spending. She's tracking where the money went. She's being responsible.

The system itself is the problem.

It demands more attention than any human being has to give it, especially at the end of a long day when you've already made a thousand decisions and your brain feels like oatmeal. You can't reconcile your way to financial peace. The tracking has to happen automatically, in the background, while you're living your actual life.

The card system I'm about to show you doesn't require you to become a different person. It doesn't demand evening reconciliation sessions or highlighters or printouts.

It works because it removes the reconciliation step entirely.

But first, let's talk about why cards feel so dangerous in the first place—because that fear isn't entirely wrong.

Cash has weight. You can feel it leave your hand. There's a physical loss when you pay for something—your wallet gets lighter, the bills disappear, the transaction is complete and irreversible. Cards feel like magic tricks. You tap or swipe, and walk away with your purchase. The money hasn't left yet. Not really. It's still there in your account, at least for now, at least until some future version of you has to deal with the consequences.

When I first started managing my own money—badly, I should add—I tried the all-cash envelope system. You stuff your budgeted amounts into physical envelopes labeled "groceries" and "gas" and "fun money," and when the envelope's empty, you're done spending in that category. Simple. Foolproof.

Except I lost an envelope.

Just straight-up lost it. One hundred twenty dollars in cash, gone somewhere between my kitchen counter and my car. I tore apart my apartment looking for it and never found it. Maybe it fell out of my bag in a parking lot. Maybe it slipped between the seats. I don't know. What I do know is that a system that depends on me not losing things was doomed from the start.

Here's what nobody tells you about cash: it's also where spending goes to die. Cash leaves no record. It evaporates. You can't review it, can't categorize it, can't learn from it. It's gone, and all you have is a vague sense that you bought...coffee? Lunch? Did you leave that $20 as a tip or spend it at the farmer's market?

Cards, used correctly, give you something cash never can: a complete, searchable, automatically categorized record of where your money went. Every transaction leaves a trail. Your bank's app does most of the work for you—it sorts purchases into "groceries," "gas," "dining," "entertainment" without you lifting a finger.

The categorization isn't perfect. My bank once classified a purchase at Panera as "home improvement," which still baffles me. But it's close enough to give you a clear picture fast.

Knowing you spent $340 on takeout last month isn't about guilt. It's about information. Maybe you're fine with that number—maybe takeout is your sanity-saver on long work nights and it's worth every penny. Or maybe you see that number and think, "Wait, $340? I thought it was like...$150, tops."

That gap between perception and reality is where your budget falls apart.

You can't close that gap if you don't see it exists. Cash keeps you blind. Cards—the right cards, used the right way—turn the lights on.

But the wrong way? The wrong way will bury you faster than cash ever could.

Debit cards pull money straight from your checking account. They're essentially digital cash—no debt risk (assuming you turn off overdraft protection, which you absolutely should), and the money leaves your account immediately.

Credit cards are where things get interesting.

The rewards are real. A good cashback card gives you 1-2% back on everything you buy, sometimes more in specific categories. Put $2,000 a month through a 2% cashback card and pay it off in full, that's $480 a year. Not life-changing money, but not nothing.

But—and this is the "but" that trips up half the people who carry credit cards—that only works if you pay your balance in full every single month.

Not most of it. Not "pretty close."

Every penny.

Credit card interest rates hover around 20-25% APR. Carry a $2,000 balance and you're paying hundreds in interest annually. Suddenly that $480 in rewards looks pretty pathetic. You're paying the credit card company to use your own money.

The people who successfully use credit cards for rewards treat them like a convenience tool, not a spending tool. They buy things they were already going to buy, on a card that gives them a small rebate for doing so. The card doesn't change the purchase decision—it just makes it slightly cheaper.

Sarah—the freelance designer we met back in Chapter 5—uses her credit card for recurring bills. Internet, phone, streaming services, the subscriptions she'd be paying for anyway. That's maybe $200 a month, all on autopay, all guaranteed to get paid in full when the bill comes. She gets her cashback. The companies get their money. Nobody's carrying a balance.

She doesn't use it for "I'll figure out how to pay for this later" purchases.

That's where trouble starts.

Credit cards give you permission to lie to yourself. That new jacket you can't quite afford? Put it on the card, deal with it next month. Dinner out when you're already over budget? Card. The kids need new shoes and you don't have the cash right now? Card.

Each individual purchase feels manageable. Defensible, even. But they add up faster than you think, and then it's three months later and you're carrying a balance that's growing every month because you can't quite pay it all off and you're not even sure how you got here.

The credit card didn't cause the problem. It just made it easy to ignore the problem until it was too late.

The key isn't willpower.

Willpower is exhausting and unreliable and runs out by 3 PM on a Tuesday when you've already made eighty decisions and someone's asking if you want to add guacamole for an extra dollar-fifty and your brain just...gives up.

The key is a system that doesn't require willpower at all.

Sarah calls it the "buffer check." Before she buys anything—online, in-store, doesn't matter—she pulls up her bank app and looks at her checking account balance. Not the total balance, but the available balance after accounting for bills that haven't cleared yet and the automatic transfers to savings that are scheduled to hit. If the purchase fits comfortably within that buffer, she buys it.

If it doesn't, she waits.

That's it.

No complex calculations, no spreadsheet formulas, no moral deliberation about whether she "deserves" the thing. Just a quick math check: Can I afford this right now, with money I actually have?

Yes or no.

This isn't deprivation. It's alignment. You're making sure your spending matches your available resources before you commit.

Some banks let you set daily spending limits on your debit card through their app. It works like a circuit breaker—it stops you before you can blow past your budget in a moment of weakness.

For credit cards, the trick is visibility.

If you check your account balance every day—or even every few days—small charges don't pile up into shocking surprises. I do this while I'm having my morning coffee. Takes maybe thirty seconds. Swipe open the app, glance at the numbers, close it.

That thirty-second habit has probably saved me thousands of dollars over the years because it keeps me honest about what I'm actually spending. Not what I think I'm spending or what I wish I was spending or what I planned to spend back when the month started and I was full of optimism.

What I'm actually spending.

That gap is everything.

Let me tell you about Michael, because his story illustrates both the danger and the solution.

Michael's a freelance photographer. His income is inconsistent—some months bring in $7,000, some bring in $2,500, and he never quite knows which one he's going to get. When he first started using credit cards, he got seduced by the rewards programs. Travel points! Cashback!

Within six months he was carrying $4,000 in credit card debt.

The rewards he'd earned? Maybe $150 worth of points.

The interest he was paying? Nearly $70 a month, and climbing.

The problem wasn't that Michael was irresponsible. The problem was he hadn't connected his card usage to his actual budget. The credit card existed in its own little universe, disconnected from the rest of his financial life, and that universe had a tendency to expand faster than he could keep up with.

He'd charge gear for a photo shoot and tell himself he'd pay it off when the client paid him. Then the client would be late, and another job would come up that needed different equipment, and suddenly he was juggling multiple purchases across multiple billing cycles and he'd lost track of what he owed and when.

The debt crept up so gradually he didn't notice it happening. A hundred here, two hundred there. None of it felt reckless in the moment.

Here's what Michael does now, three years debt-free:

He estimates his average monthly expenses—fixed and variable—and sets a credit card spending limit slightly below that amount. Not the credit limit the bank gives him, but his own internal limit based on what he can actually afford to pay off.

He set up an automatic payment to pay the full statement balance every month, scheduled for two days before the due date. This is non-negotiable. If the money isn't there to cover the full balance, he doesn't use the card that month.

But the real genius of Michael's system is this: he treats his credit card like a virtual envelope system.

He's got mental categories—groceries, gear, entertainment, business expenses—and every time he makes a purchase, he immediately logs it in a simple note on his phone. Not a fancy app, not a spreadsheet, just a running list.

"Groceries: $87. Gear: $240. Entertainment: $45."

He knows how much he's allocated to each category, and when he's getting close to the limit, he sees it in real time. If he's about to blow past his grocery budget, he knows he'll need to compensate somewhere else—maybe skip the concert this month, or dip into his "fun money" envelope. The card isn't giving him infinite spending power. It's just a more convenient way to track the same envelope limits he'd use with cash.

And he's strategic about rewards. He redeems points for travel expenses he's already budgeted for, which effectively reduces those costs.

The rewards are a bonus, not a justification.

That shift—from "I earned these points so I deserve this trip" to "I was already taking this trip and the points made it cheaper"—sounds subtle, but it changes everything. One mindset inflates your lifestyle. The other one funds it sustainably.

So how do you actually implement this for yourself?

Start with an honest assessment. Pull up your most recent credit card statement—or the last three months if you really want to see the pattern. Are you paying the balance in full every month?

If not, that's your first priority. Not because I'm judging you, but because carrying a balance turns your rewards card into an expensive loan.

Look at where your money is actually going. Most banks and credit card companies give you spending breakdowns by category—dining, groceries, gas, entertainment. This isn't about shame. It's about data. You can't change a pattern you don't see.

Then set realistic limits for yourself. Not aspirational "I wish I only spent this much" limits—realistic "I can actually stick to this" limits. Pick one or two categories where you tend to overspend and focus there first.

And here's the part that makes it all work: automate as much as possible.

Set up automatic payments for your credit card bills. Link your accounts to your bank's app so you can see real-time updates. The goal isn't to eliminate cards from your life—it's to integrate them into a system that actually serves you.

Most budgeting apps are overkill. They connect to seventeen accounts, generate beautiful charts, send you notifications about every $4 coffee purchase. For most people, that's not helpful—it's just noise. Your bank's app already shows you what you spent and where. That's usually enough.

Don't overcomplicate this. The best budget is the one you'll actually use.

Now let's talk about the real power move: dedicated cards for specific categories.

Instead of one card for everything—where you're constantly trying to mentally sort which charge was for what—you assign specific cards to specific spending envelopes. Groceries on one card. Gas and car stuff on another. Entertainment and dining on a third.

I know how this sounds. It sounds like more complexity, more accounts to manage, more cards cluttering your wallet. But here's what it actually does: it makes categorization automatic.

When your grocery card statement arrives, you know exactly what that bill represents. You're not scrolling through trying to figure out which Target trip was groceries and which was the birthday present and which was the impulse buy you're trying to forget about.

It's already sorted. The mental load drops to almost nothing.

Sarah has four cards:

Groceries & Household **Transportation** (gas, car maintenance, parking) **Creative Expenses** (art supplies, software, fonts, anything work-related) **Fun Money** (dining out, movies, concerts, the stuff that makes life worth living)

When she buys groceries, she uses the Groceries card. Tank of gas? Transportation. New brush set for a project? Creative Expenses. Date night? Fun Money.

This isn't about restriction. It's about clarity. She still buys all the same things—she just knows, instantly and without effort, how much she's spending in each area. When the statement arrives she can see: "Okay, I spent $280 on groceries this month, $140 on gas, $95 on creative supplies, and $160 on fun stuff."

If one of those numbers looks high, she adjusts next month. If they all look fine, she moves on with her life.

What about purchases that could fit in multiple categories? Sarah buys a desk chair for her home office—is that Household or Creative Expenses?

Pick one. It doesn't matter which.

The goal isn't perfect accounting—it's consistent categorization. Sarah usually defaults to whichever category feels more primary. A desk chair is mostly for work, so it goes on Creative Expenses. Done.

No agonizing, no splitting the charge, no second-guessing. The perfectionism trap is real, and it will kill your budget faster than overspending will.

And cash? Cash is your "miscellaneous" envelope. If you pull out $20 for a farmers market trip or a cash-only food truck, it comes out of that general pot. You can't track it as precisely, which is fine—minimize cash spending where possible, and don't stress about the occasional small cash purchase.

The beauty of the dedicated card approach is that it removes the guesswork. You're not trying to remember what you bought or which category it belonged to or whether that Amazon order was books for work or kitchen stuff for home. The card you used tells you. Instantly. Automatically.

This is what I mean when I say the best budget is the one that requires the least amount of your attention. You're not tracking your spending. Your cards are tracking it for you.

The real magic happens when you connect this card system to your monthly budget—the three-envelope framework we built back in Chapters 3 and 4.

Each card corresponds to an envelope. Each envelope has a spending limit. When the statement arrives, you compare what you actually spent against what you budgeted.

If you budgeted $300 for groceries and only charged $265, you're $35 ahead. You can roll that forward, move it to another envelope, or save it. Your call.

If you overspent by $40? That's information, not failure. Maybe you had a birthday party to host and needed extra supplies—fine, totally reasonable. Or maybe you've been stress-buying snacks and didn't realize it until you saw the number.

Either way, now you know. You can adjust next month.

Here's how to set this up:

First, list your major expense categories. The envelopes we defined earlier in the book—groceries, transportation, housing costs, debt payments, fun money, whatever fits your life.

Second, decide which cards you'll dedicate to which categories. You don't need a card for every single envelope—group related expenses where it makes sense. Transportation costs (gas, parking, Uber, car repairs) can all live on one card. Household stuff (groceries, cleaning supplies, home maintenance) on another.

Third, physically label your cards if it helps. A small sticker on the back that says "GROCERIES" prevents you from accidentally grabbing the wrong one at checkout. Sounds silly, but it works.

Fourth, set calendar reminders to review each statement when it arrives. This isn't a punishment—it's feedback. You're looking for patterns, not perfection. Did you stay within your limits? Great. Did you go over? Why? What adjustments do you need to make?

The system isn't meant to constrict you. It's meant to give you clarity so you can make intentional choices instead of wondering where the hell all your money went.

Jennifer—remember her from the beginning of this chapter?—switched to dedicated cards six months ago. She's got three: one for household expenses (groceries, Target runs, household supplies), one for kids' stuff (clothes, activities, school expenses), and one for everything else (date nights, her own purchases, the random stuff that doesn't fit elsewhere).

Last month she sat down to review her statements and it took her eleven minutes. Total.

She knew exactly where her money went. No highlighter. No detective work. No tears at the kitchen table at 10:47 PM.

She spent $340 on household stuff, $180 on kid expenses, and $210 on everything else. The numbers matched her budget almost perfectly. When she saw that the "everything else" card was a bit high, she knew why—her sister's birthday dinner—and she didn't stress about it because she'd planned for occasional spikes.

The system gave her something she hadn't had in years: peace of mind.

Not because she'd become some financial wizard or developed superhuman discipline. Because the system itself was doing the work for her.

That's the whole point. You shouldn't have to think about your budget every single day. You shouldn't have to track every transaction manually or reconcile receipts or wonder if you can afford something.

The cards track it. The envelopes contain it. The automatic payments execute it.

You just live your life.

And once a month—maybe while you're having coffee on a Sunday morning—you check in, see how you did, make any needed adjustments, and move on.

That's it.

That's the system.

Jennifer looked up from her screen, defeated. The numbers blurred together—it wasn't just money she was losing; she was losing hours of her life to this endless cycle.

Chapter 8: Troubleshooting Common Issues

I once overdrew my checking account by $180 while I had over $2,000 sitting in savings. The car made a noise—the grinding, metal-on-metal shriek that means you're pulling over *right now*.

We've become so accustomed to frictionless spending that we've lost the connection between our actions and their consequences. It's as if hitting 'pay now' absolves us of any further thought.

The car made a noise. Not the kind you ignore—the grinding, metal-on-metal shriek that means you're pulling over *right now*. I called the shop from a strip-mall parking lot, hazards on. They said it'd be around $650, maybe more once they got it on the lift. I had the money. That wasn't the problem.

The problem was my budget spreadsheet.

I'd built this elaborate system over months. Color-coded categories that shifted from green to yellow to red based on spending thresholds. Formulas that auto-calculated percentages. Five linked tabs tracking different accounts—checking, savings, two credit cards, and a "slush fund" I'd created for reasons I could no longer remember. And standing there in that parking lot with my phone battery at 4%, I couldn't figure out which account to pull from.

Checking was low because I'd just moved $800 into high-yield savings the day before. But how much of that was earmarked for what? The savings account held money for irregular bills, next month's rent, and an emergency fund I was slowly building. To know how much was actually available, I'd have to open the spreadsheet, cross-reference three tabs, and check the mental notes I'd been keeping in a separate app.

The mechanic wanted a decision. My battery was dying. I made a guess, swiped my debit card, and hoped for the best.

The overdraft fee hit the next morning. Negative $180 in the account. I transferred money to cover everything, paid the fee, and then sat at my kitchen table feeling like an idiot. This system was supposed to make my life *easier*. Instead, I'd built something so complex that I couldn't use it when it actually mattered.

And here's the thing nobody tells you about the moment a budget system fails: there's no alarm. No warning light. It happens quietly. A purchase you forget to log. An envelope you raid because you can't remember what you'd allocated. A spreadsheet you stop opening because just thinking about it makes you tired. A month where you tell yourself you'll catch up later, and then later never comes.

You don't fail because you overspent. You fail because the system asked you to think, and you were too busy living your life to comply.

That $180 overdraft fee was expensive. But the real cost—the one that took me longer to recognize—was the weeks I spent after that just... not budgeting at all. I abandoned the spreadsheet. Went back to checking my account balance before purchases and hoping I was remembering everything correctly. I told myself I'd rebuild the system when things calmed down.

Things didn't calm down. They never do.

For three months I lived in that fog where you're not quite sure what you can afford, so you say no to things you could've enjoyed and yes to things you'll regret. I missed a friend's birthday dinner because I wasn't confident I had the money. Two weeks later I impulse-bought a $90 jacket I wore once. When you don't have clarity, you make bad choices in both directions.

The system broke. But the breaking didn't cost me $180. It cost me three months of financial confidence, plus however much money I lost to that fog of bad decisions. I'll never know the exact number, which is somehow worse.

If you've ever had a budget system fall apart on you, you know this feeling. The way the failure creeps in. How long you go before you even admit it's not working anymore. The guilt that sits on you like weight.

And if your system hasn't fallen apart yet, it will. Not because you're undisciplined. Because every system has edges, and eventually you'll hit one.

The car that needs immediate repair. The month where groceries just cost more. The family emergency that requires a plane ticket you didn't budget for. The birthday party with an entry fee. The prescription that isn't covered. The parking ticket. The broken phone. The leak under the sink.

Life doesn't care about your envelope system.

The question isn't whether you'll hit an edge. It's whether you have a plan for what happens when you do.

Most people don't. They improvise. They guess. They reach for a credit card and tell themselves they'll pay it off next month. Sometimes they do. More often, that balance sits there, accruing interest, while they try to figure out why the budget isn't working anymore.

So let's talk about what actually breaks, and what you do about it before you're standing in a parking lot making expensive guesses.

The biggest issue most people face isn't the Needs envelope. You pay rent or you don't have a place to live. That clarity keeps you honest.

It's the Wants envelope that becomes the black hole.

The category that's supposed to be fun—the one that's supposed to make the whole system feel less like deprivation—turns into this monthly guilt trip where you're consistently over budget. You set $300 aside. By the fifteenth, it's gone. You promise yourself you'll do better next month. Next month looks exactly the same. You start to wonder if you're just bad at this, if maybe some people are wired for budgeting and you're not one of them.

I know what you're thinking: "Just spend less on wants."

Right. Helpful.

The problem isn't that you don't *know* you're overspending. You're not stupid. You can see the envelope draining faster than it should. The problem is that "spend less" isn't a strategy. It's a wish. And wishes don't change behavior.

Here's what actually works: catch the pattern *before* the money is spent.

Start by identifying your hotspot. Not "wants" as a whole—that's too broad, too easy to wave away. The specific subcategory where money evaporates fastest. For some people it's dining out. For others it's clothing, or books that pile up unread, or craft supplies that get used once and buried in a closet, or plants that die within a month because you forgot you're not actually good at keeping things alive.

You need to know your leak. Not guess. Know.

Track it for two weeks if you have to. Every purchase, write down the category. At the end of the two weeks, look at where the money actually went. You'll see it. The one area that keeps showing up, over and over, until you can't ignore it anymore.

Once you've identified it, apply the 24-Hour Rule.

The rule is simple: if you see something you want to buy—anything beyond everyday essentials—you wait 24 hours before purchasing it.

Just one day.

I started doing this after I realized I'd bought three different yoga mats in six months. Three. I didn't need three yoga mats. I didn't even do yoga that often. But I'd see one on sale, or in a color I liked, and I'd buy it in the moment because it *felt* like a good decision. Twenty-four hours later, I would've remembered I already owned two.

What happens in that waiting period is that your brain stops being flooded with dopamine and starts asking practical questions. Do I actually need this? Where will I put it? Didn't I just buy something similar last month? Will I still want this tomorrow, or is this just the particular emotional state I'm in right now?

The vast majority of impulse purchases die in that waiting period.

I'm not exaggerating. I'd estimate that 70% of the things I add to online carts never get purchased once I impose the 24-hour wait. They just sit there until I close the browser tab and forget they ever existed. That's money I didn't spend on things I didn't actually want.

But let's say the want survives. You wait the full 24 hours and you still want it. You've thought about it. It's not just impulse. Now you look for a cheaper alternative.

This works especially well for recurring indulgences.

A woman I know—Sarah, worked in project management at a tech company—loved getting her nails done every two weeks. Full set, gel polish, the works. $70 each visit. That's $140 a month, $1,680 a year. It wasn't *wrong* to enjoy that. Nobody's saying you can't have nice things. But it was eating her Wants envelope alive, and every month she'd look at that category and feel like she was failing.

She didn't eliminate it. That would've felt like punishment, and punishment doesn't stick. Instead, she bought a decent at-home gel kit for $80—watched YouTube tutorials until she got the hang of it—and started doing her own nails most of the time. She kept salon visits for special occasions, maybe once every six weeks. Birthdays. Important work presentations. Dates where she wanted to feel particularly put-together.

The savings were immediate. The resentment? Nonexistent. She was still getting her nails done. Just differently.

That's the trade-down approach. You're not eliminating joy. You're finding a version of the same joy that costs less.

My brother Mark did this with his daily Starbucks run. Grande caramel macchiato, every morning, $5.50 after tip. He had the routine down: leave the house at 7:18, hit the drive-through, arrive at work by 7:35 with a hot coffee in hand. It was part of his identity. That's $165 a month, nearly $2,000 a year.

He didn't quit coffee. He bought a decent espresso machine—found a used Breville on Facebook Marketplace for $180—and started making lattes at home most mornings. He still hit Starbucks on Fridays, kept it as a treat. The ritual still existed; it was just less frequent. Monthly coffee spending dropped to around $40.

But here's the deeper question, the one most budgeting advice doesn't ask: *why* are you making those impulse purchases in the first place?

Boredom? Stress? Trying to fill some emotional gap that has nothing to do with actually needing a new sweater or another book you won't read or a subscription box full of things you didn't know existed until an ad showed you?

The pattern matters more than the individual purchase.

I knew a woman named Lisa who worked in marketing. She kept overspending on clothes. Not just a little over. She'd set a $100 monthly budget and regularly hit $400, sometimes more. The closet was full of things with tags still on them. Dresses she'd worn once to feel better about buying them, then never again. Shoes in her size but not really her style, purchased because they were on sale and she could justify the deal even if she couldn't justify the need.

She tried the 24-hour rule. She tried cheaper alternatives—thrift stores, Poshmark, borrowing from friends. Nothing stuck. Every month, the same overage. Every month, the same guilt.

Then she started tracking *when* the purchases happened.

Not just what or how much. When.

Almost every shopping binge came after a particularly stressful day at work. She wasn't buying clothes because she needed them. She wasn't even buying them because she wanted them, not really. She was buying them because clicking "purchase" gave her a hit of control in a life that felt chaotic. Three difficult meetings with a boss who kept moving the goalposts? New dress in her cart by evening. Presentation that went badly? Two pairs of shoes ordered before she even got home.

Once she saw the pattern, she could interrupt it.

Started going to yoga classes after rough workdays instead of opening retail apps. Scheduled coffee dates with friends for decompression instead of mall trips. Called her sister and vented for 20 minutes instead of scrolling through sales. The clothing budget stabilized almost immediately—not perfectly, not every month, but close enough that she stopped feeling like she was fighting a losing battle.

You might be thinking, "Okay, but what if I'm *already* doing all of this and I'm still overspending?"

Then the issue isn't impulse control. It's allocation.

You've underestimated how much you actually need—or want—to spend in that category. And this is where people get stuck, because they feel like admitting they need *more* in the Wants envelope is failure.

It's not. It's honesty.

If you're consistently running $50 over budget each month even after applying every strategy in this chapter—24-hour rule, trade-downs, addressing the emotional triggers—then the number is wrong. You don't need more discipline. You need a different number.

I'd rather adjust the allocation and succeed than keep the same allocation and fail every month while hating myself for it.

But if you're going to increase Wants, something else has to give. Money is finite. You can't add $50 to Wants without subtracting it from somewhere else. Maybe that means temporarily reducing savings—not eliminating it, just slowing the pace. Maybe it means cutting back on another discretionary category you care about less. Maybe it means you need to bring in more income, whether that's a side project or negotiating a raise or selling things you don't use.

Think of it like adjusting sails on a boat. You don't set them once at the dock and hope for the best all the way across the lake. You make constant small corrections based on wind, current, weather. Your budget should be equally responsive. Rigid budgets break. Flexible ones bend and hold.

Perfection is not the goal. Everyone overshoots a category sometimes. The difference between someone who makes a system work and someone who gives up is what happens *after* the overspending. Do you analyze it, adjust, and keep going? Or do you decide the whole thing is pointless and abandon ship?

If you blow the Wants budget one month, don't throw the envelopes in a drawer and go back to swiping blindly. Figure out what triggered it. Make a plan for next month. Keep going.

Now let's talk about the thing that derails even the most disciplined budgeters: unexpected expenses.

Not the small stuff—the parking meter you forgot to feed, the $12 late fee on a library book. I'm talking about the car repair that costs $1,200. The emergency vet bill when your dog eats something he shouldn't have. The laptop that dies three days before a major work deadline and you can't wait for a sale.

These aren't theoretical. If you've been alive for more than a few years, you've already lived through several of these moments. The sudden jolt of a necessary expense you didn't see coming. The sick feeling in your stomach as you realize this is going to hurt.

You'll live through more.

The question isn't whether they'll happen. It's whether you have a plan that doesn't involve panic and a credit card.

This is where the Buffer envelope earns its keep. You've been deliberately under-allocating to it all along, letting small amounts accumulate month after month. It's been sitting there quietly, ignored, not particularly exciting. When an unexpected expense hits and it's within the buffer amount, you're covered. Transfer the money, handle the bill, move on with your day. No drama.

But what happens when the expense is *bigger* than your buffer?

Let's say Maria—a graphic designer I met at a conference a few years back—has been using the envelope system for three months. She's diligent about it. Tracks everything. She's got $250 in her Buffer envelope. Not a fortune, but more than she's ever had set aside before. Then her car needs $800 in repairs. Transmission issue. Not fixable with duct tape and hope.

That's a $550 gap.

Her first instinct—like most people, like probably you if you're honest—is to reach for a credit card. It's right there in her wallet. The mechanic takes Visa. She could have this problem solved in 30 seconds and deal with it later.

Don't.

Not yet.

Look at the other envelopes first. Not the ones funding absolute necessities like rent and utilities. Those stay untouched unless you're facing a genuine survival emergency, the kind where you're choosing between housing and everything else. I'm talking about the discretionary categories. Fun Money. Dining Out. Clothing. Hobbies. Subscriptions. The categories that make life pleasant but aren't keeping you alive.

Could you temporarily reduce funding to those areas?

Maria looked at her setup. She'd been allocating $150 a month to dining out—not extravagant, just enough to meet friends for dinner once a week and grab lunch out on Fridays. But for the next three months, she could trim that to $50. Pack lunch most days. Meet friends for coffee instead of dinner. That freed up $100 a month, or $300 over three months.

She also had a $200 clothing envelope. But she didn't *need* new clothes right now. Her closet was full. She could postpone that spending entirely for a couple months. Another $400 total.

Her hobbies envelope—$100 a month for art supplies, since she painted on weekends—could drop to $50 temporarily. She had enough materials stockpiled to keep working. That's another $50 this month, $150 over three.

Add it up: $300 from dining out, $400 from clothing, $150 from hobbies, plus the $250 already in her buffer. That's $1,100. More than enough to cover the $800 repair without touching a credit card. She'd still have $300 left over.

You might be thinking this sounds like deprivation. Like punishment.

It's not. It's triage.

The key word is *temporary*. Maria isn't eliminating dining out or hobbies forever. She's not declaring that she'll never buy clothes again. She's recognizing that a necessary expense has appeared—something genuinely unavoidable, not a want disguised as a need—and making short-term adjustments in less critical areas to cover it. Once the buffer is replenished, she can restore those other envelopes to normal levels.

This is the difference between a system that bends and one that breaks.

Rigid systems say, "You have $250 in your buffer and the expense is $800, so you're screwed. Hope you like credit card debt." Flexible systems say, "You have $250 in your buffer, plus discretionary spending across four other envelopes that can be temporarily reduced. Let's make it work."

But what about expenses that aren't sudden but also aren't small?

Car registration due in three months: $250. You know it's coming. It's not an emergency. The DMV sent you a notice. But it also doesn't fit neatly into any existing envelope, and if you ignore it until it's due, you'll be scrambling to pull together $250 all at once while also funding that month's regular expenses.

The solution is to create a temporary envelope specifically for that expense and fund it gradually.

Allocate $85 a month for the next three months, and by the time registration is due, the money is sitting there waiting. No scrambling. No stress. No suddenly realizing the day before that you're $250 short and you'll have to pull from somewhere else.

This same principle applies to anything you can see coming: holidays, birthdays, annual subscriptions, vacations, professional development courses, gifts for weddings you've already been invited to.

If you know it's on the horizon, start setting aside small amounts now.

I did this last year with Christmas. I know—everyone *knows*—that Christmas happens in December. Every single year, same date, no surprises. And yet somehow it always felt like this expense that appeared out of nowhere. I'd get to mid-December and suddenly realize I needed to buy gifts for twelve people, plus travel to see family, plus contribute to the office party fund, plus all the random holiday expenses that pop up when you're not paying attention.

Every year I told myself I'd plan better. Every year I didn't.

So in September—three months out—I created a temporary envelope. Started putting $150 a month into it. By December I had $600 set aside specifically for gifts, travel, the random holiday expenses. For the first time in years, I got through the holidays without that sinking feeling of watching my checking account drain in real time while I tried to calculate whether I could afford one more gift or if I'd already gone too far.

The money was just there. Waiting. Ready.

And sometimes, despite all of this planning, you'll still miscalculate. You'll underestimate an expense or overestimate your ability to cut back elsewhere. Maybe you'll just have a bad month where everything costs more than you expected and you can't quite figure out why.

When that happens—and it will, because you're human and humans miscalculate—don't treat it as proof that you're bad with money or that the system doesn't work.

Treat it as data.

What went wrong? Was your initial estimate unrealistic—did you budget $400 for groceries when your actual typical spending is closer to $500? Did an unexpected trigger lead to impulse spending you didn't see coming? Were there circumstances genuinely beyond your control, like a price increase on something you buy regularly or a surprise expense you couldn't have predicted?

Once you've identified the root cause, adjust for next month. Maybe you need to increase allocation to a particular envelope because your original estimate was based on wishful thinking rather than reality. Maybe you need to build your buffer faster so you have more cushion when things go sideways. Maybe you need to have an honest conversation with yourself about whether your current income can actually support your current lifestyle, or if something bigger has to change.

This isn't failure. It's iteration.

Every month you run this system, you get better at predicting your actual spending patterns and adjusting allocations accordingly. The envelopes aren't meant to create anxiety. They're tools for clarity. And clarity improves with practice.

There's another issue that creeps in gradually, so slowly you don't notice until the whole system feels off: envelope drift.

It starts innocently.

You're at the grocery store and you grab paper towels. You pay with the Groceries envelope because, well, you bought them at the grocery store. Makes sense. Then you're there again next week and you pick up dog food because it's on sale and you might as well stock up. Also goes on the Groceries envelope.

A few weeks later, you're looking at your budget and wondering why Groceries is always over while Household Supplies and Pet Care both have surpluses. You can't figure out what changed. You feel like you're buying the same things you always buy.

You are. You're just funding two or three categories out of one envelope without realizing it.

This seems like a small thing. A few dollars shifted here and there. Who cares, as long as the total spending is under control?

But those small shifts obscure the actual data you're trying to collect. The whole *point* of separating envelopes is to see where money is really going—not just how much you're spending total, but specifically where. If you're constantly blurring the lines between categories, you lose that clarity. You can't make good decisions about where to cut back or where you might need to allocate more, because the numbers are all mixed up.

The fix is to re-establish clear boundaries for each envelope.

And don't be afraid to redefine those boundaries if your original categories aren't working. The categories aren't sacred. They're not handed down from some budgeting authority. They're tools you created, and tools can be reshaped when they stop fitting.

Maybe you initially separated "Coffee Shops" from "Dining Out," thinking you'd want to track them independently. But in practice you can never remember which envelope to use when you grab a sandwich at the café. Is that dining out, or is it a coffee shop purchase because you bought it at a café? You waste time deliberating over a $9 transaction, and that's not a good use of your mental energy.

Combine them into one "Food Away From Home" envelope. Problem solved.

Or maybe "Personal Care" has become this catch-all that includes everything from haircuts to toothpaste to the gym membership to new running shoes, and you're realizing those are very different types of expenses with different frequencies and different levels of necessity. A haircut every six weeks is not the same as toothpaste you buy monthly is not the same as running shoes you replace twice a year.

Split it. "Salon & Services" and "Toiletries & Household" and "Fitness." Now you have useful data instead of a muddled catch-all.

You might be thinking, "But doesn't changing categories all the time defeat the purpose of tracking? How can I see trends if I keep redefining what I'm measuring?"

Only if you're changing them randomly, on a whim, every month for no clear reason.

If you're refining them based on actual spending patterns—making the system fit your life instead of trying to force your life into arbitrary boxes someone else designed—that's not chaos. That's learning. That's the system getting better.

Another place drift happens is with the temptation to "borrow" from future envelopes.

You're out of money in your Gas envelope, but payday isn't for another week. You think, "I'll just take $30 from next month's Gas allocation. I'll fill up now, and when I get paid I'll put the money back. I'll be fine."

Except now you've created a hole in next month's budget before it even starts.

You're essentially going into debt *within your own system*. And if next month is tight for any reason—if an unexpected expense pops up, or if you overspend in another category—you're starting from behind, which makes it even harder to catch up. You'll be tempted to borrow again. Then again. Then you're in this cycle where you're perpetually one step behind your own budget, constantly scrambling to patch holes you created yourself.

This is one of those things that seems harmless in the moment but becomes a vicious cycle fast. I've seen it happen. I've done it myself.

Don't borrow from future envelopes. If you're out of money in a category, you're out. Either shift funds from a different *current* envelope—something happening in the same month, where you can see the trade-off clearly—or wait until you can afford the purchase.

It's harsh. I know it feels harsh. But it's the only way the system holds.

The moment you start borrowing from the future, you're back to the same mental accounting tricks that got you into trouble before you had envelopes at all.

Let me tell you about a friend named Sarah—different from the other Sarahs I've mentioned, a middle school teacher in Ohio—who started using this system after years of feeling like her money just evaporated every month.

She set up her envelopes carefully. Rent, utilities, groceries, transportation, entertainment, clothing, dining out. Everything had a place. She was meticulous about it—tracked every purchase, reconciled the envelopes weekly, felt like she finally had control after years of financial fog.

The first month went smoothly. She stayed within every category. Had money left over at the end, which she'd never experienced before. She felt more in control than she had in years, maybe ever.

Then her sister called.

Destination wedding. Three months away. Cancun. Sarah was thrilled—she loved her sister, they'd always been close—and also immediately stressed, because she hadn't budgeted for travel, or a wedding gift, or the kind of outfit you wear to a beach wedding in Mexico, or the various incidentals that pile up around a trip like that.

Her first move was to raid other envelopes. Pulled $150 from Groceries because she figured she could eat cheaper for a couple weeks. Pulled $80 from Household Supplies because she didn't *need* to replace anything right now. Even dipped into her small emergency fund for $200, telling herself this kind of counted as an emergency.

Within two weeks, everything was chaos.

She'd pulled so much from Groceries that she didn't have enough left to actually feed herself properly, which meant she was eating out more, which meant Dining Out was also over budget. She ran out of cleaning supplies and had to buy more, but that money had already been reallocated. Her laundry detergent ran out. She needed new toothpaste. Small things, but they added up, and she didn't have the budget for them anymore.

It felt like playing whack-a-mole. Every fix created a new problem.

She got stressed. Started avoiding the envelopes entirely because looking at them made her feel worse. Spent three weeks just swiping her card and hoping things would somehow work out.

Then she stopped, took a breath, and actually looked at the envelopes without panicking.

She made some hard choices.

Clothing envelope: reduced to near-zero for three months. She didn't love it, but she had enough to wear. Nothing was falling apart. She could pause. Entertainment envelope: cut in half. She'd been going to movies and concerts regularly; she could pause that temporarily. Streaming subscriptions she barely used: canceled.

Dining out: minimal, just enough for one meal out per month instead of weekly dinners with friends.

She created a new temporary envelope specifically for the wedding and started funding it aggressively with the money she'd freed up from those cuts.

$200 a month for three months. By the time the wedding came, she'd have $600, plus the money she'd already pulled from other places. Enough to cover the flight, the hotel, the gift, the dress. Not lavish, but enough.

It wasn't comfortable. She missed the concerts. Missed going out to dinner. But it was intentional. She knew exactly what she was sacrificing and why, and she knew it was temporary. Three months. Then back to normal.

Three months later, she went to the wedding. Had a great time. Danced at the reception, cried during the vows, spent a long weekend on a beach with her sister and their extended family. Came home without a dollar of credit card debt.

The week after she got back, she restored her other envelopes to normal levels and kept going.

That's what a functioning system looks like when life throws something unexpected at it. Not perfection. Not ease. Just the ability to bend without breaking. The willingness to make hard choices for a defined period of time, and then return to normal.

\---

One more thing, because it comes up often enough that it's worth addressing directly: what if you just... forget?

What if you're three weeks into the month and you realize you haven't been tracking purchases properly, and now you have no idea which envelope you've been spending from?

First: breathe. This is fixable.

Go through your bank statements and credit card transactions for the past three weeks. It'll take maybe 20 minutes. Reconstruct where the money went. Assign each purchase to the appropriate envelope retroactively.

Yes, it's annoying. Yes, you'll wish you'd just tracked it properly in the first place. But 20 minutes of retroactive tracking is better than abandoning the whole system because you missed a few weeks.

Once you're caught up, look at why you stopped tracking. Was the method too cumbersome—were you trying to log every purchase in a complicated app that required twelve taps and a Wi-Fi connection? Was it taking too long? Did life just get busy and you forgot?

If the method is the problem, simplify it. Maybe you switch to a notes app on your phone where you can jot down purchases in five seconds. Maybe you keep paper receipts and reconcile once a week instead of logging in real time. Maybe you set a daily reminder at 8 PM to do a quick mental review of what you spent that day.

If you just forgot because life got hectic, set up external reminders. A recurring calendar notification. A sticky note on your bathroom mirror. A habit stack where you always check your envelopes right after you pour your morning coffee.

The system only works if you use it. But using it doesn't have to be complicated. It just has to happen.

Most budgeting systems fail not because they're bad systems, but because they demand more attention than you have to give. If tracking every purchase feels like a part-time job, you won't do it. And if you don't do it, the system collapses.

This is why I keep saying: complexity is a tax. Every extra step, every additional category, every formula that requires cross-referencing three tabs—those aren't features. They're friction. And friction kills momentum.

The best system is the one you'll actually use when you're tired, when you're busy, when life is happening and you don't have time to think. If your system requires you to sit down with a spreadsheet for 30 minutes every Saturday, it will eventually fail. Maybe not this month. Maybe not next month. But eventually you'll have a busy Saturday, and then another, and then you'll be three weeks behind and the whole thing will feel insurmountable.

So whatever troubleshooting you do—whatever fixes you apply to the issues I've laid out in this chapter—make sure the fix doesn't add complexity. Make sure it doesn't require more of your attention.

If overspending in the Wants envelope is your issue, the fix isn't to create seven subcategories so you can track wants more precisely. That's more work. The fix is the 24-hour rule, which requires no additional tracking.

If unexpected expenses are derailing you, the fix isn't a detailed predictive model of every possible thing that could go wrong. The fix is a buffer you fund gradually, and a plan for temporarily reducing discretionary spending when something big hits.

If envelope drift is blurring your data, the fix isn't more categories. It's clearer boundaries on the categories you already have, or combining categories that overlap.

Simple fixes. Ones that reduce mental load instead of increasing it.

Because here's the truth most personal finance advice won't tell you: your attention is more scarce than your money. You have a limited amount of mental energy to spend on budgeting, and if the system demands more than you have, it doesn't matter how theoretically perfect it is. You won't use it.

The system that works is the one that fits your life as it actually is, not as you wish it were. The one that bends when you hit an edge, instead of shattering and leaving you back where you started.

Now you know what breaks, and what to do when it does. The question is whether you'll wait until something breaks to apply these fixes—or whether you'll build the flexibility in now, before you need it.

The grinding noise sounded less like a mechanical failure and more like an alarm bell, signaling that the true cost of inaction was far greater than any repair bill.

Chapter 9: Putting It All Together: The 'Set and Forget' System

It's 10:47 on a Sunday night. You're sitting at your laptop with a knot in your stomach, staring at three browser tabs—your bank account, your budgeting app, and a half-finished Excel sheet you promised yourself you'd update weekly. You haven't touched it in seventeen days.

The system isn't about deprivation—it's about recognizing that contentment doesn't come from accumulating more, but from making conscious choices with what we already have. Those original white envelopes weren't fancy, but they held a quiet power: intention.

My grandmother's Friday night ritual with her white envelopes took maybe twenty minutes a week. This system takes five minutes a month. Same principle: decide once, then the money knows where it belongs.

But here's what you won't admit out loud: you're exhausted just *thinking* about it.

That's the hidden cost nobody talks about when they hand you a budgeting system. Not the dollars you might overspend. The *attention* tax. The mental overhead of remembering to check, to update, to reconcile, to care—every single week, forever. It's not that you're lazy. It's that your attention is the scarcest resource you have, and most budgets demand a weekly tithe of it that you simply can't sustain.

I know because I've been that person at 10:47 pm, cursor blinking in an empty cell, wondering if I'm supposed to categorize the work lunch as "Dining Out" or "Networking" and whether it even matters.

The answer is: it doesn't. Not if the system itself is designed to fail.

If a budgeting approach requires more than five minutes a week to maintain, it *will* collapse. Not might. Will. And it won't be your fault—it'll be the system's fault for asking more of your brain than your brain has to give.

That's why we're building something different here. Something that doesn't require you to be a different person than you are. Something that runs on automation and rhythm instead of willpower and spreadsheet formulas. I call it the 'Set and Forget' system, and the entire philosophy rests on one idea: your budget should work *for* you in the background, not demand constant feeding and care like some high-maintenance pet.

Let's start with the foundation—automation. Not as a nice-to-have. As the *only* way this works.

You've already set up your Needs, Wants, and Savings envelopes, whether they're actual physical envelopes in a drawer or digital accounts on your phone. You know roughly how much goes into each one per month. Now we're going to make that happen without you having to *remember* it happens.

Most banks let you schedule recurring transfers. If you get paid biweekly, set up an automatic transfer every payday—the moment the money hits your checking account, a chunk moves to Needs, a chunk to Wants, a chunk to Savings. You never see it. You never decide. It just *goes*.

Here's why that matters. Willpower is a terrible budgeting tool. Willpower is what you have at 8 am on a Monday when you're fresh and optimistic. Willpower is *not* what you have at 9 pm on a Thursday when you're scrolling your phone and an ad for those boots you've been eyeing pops up and there's a sale and free shipping and your thumb is already moving toward "Buy Now."

Automation doesn't run out. Willpower does.

Let's say your Needs envelope requires fifteen hundred dollars a month. That's $375 a week if you get paid weekly, or $750 every two weeks if that's your rhythm. Schedule the transfer. Same for Wants and Savings—whatever breakdown you decided on back in Chapter 3. The money moves *before* you have a chance to spend it on something else. Before you even think about it.

I'm not saying this to sound preachy. I'm saying it because I spent two years trying to manually move money around "when I remembered" and I can count on one hand the number of months I actually did it consistently. Twice. I did it twice. The rest of the time I just... didn't. And then I'd feel bad about not doing it, which made me want to avoid looking at my budget entirely, which made the whole thing worse.

Automation breaks that cycle. You set it once. It runs forever. Done.

Now—the weekly check-in. And I know what you're already thinking: "Didn't you just say this was supposed to be low-maintenance?"

I did. And it is. Ten minutes. Maybe fifteen if something weird happened. That's it.

Here's what the check-in is *not*: a forensic audit of every transaction. You're not reconciling receipts. You're not color-coding categories. You're not building pivot tables. You're asking yourself three questions:

1. Am I still on track in each envelope? 2. Did anything unexpected happen this week? 3. Do I need to make a small adjustment?

That's it. Grab your envelopes—physical or digital—and glance at the balances. If your Needs envelope was supposed to have $450 left by now and it's got $380, you notice. You don't panic. You just *notice*. Maybe you overspent on groceries because you hosted friends for dinner. Fine. That's information. Maybe next week you pack lunch a few extra days, or you pull thirty bucks from Wants to cover the gap.

The goal isn't perfection. It's *awareness*.

I think of it like checking your mirrors while you're driving. You're not stopping the car every five minutes to measure your exact distance from the lane markers. You just glance up, make sure you're still where you're supposed to be, and if you've drifted a little, you adjust. That's the weekly check-in. A glance. An adjustment. Keep moving.

Let me show you what this looks like in practice. Sarah—freelance graphic designer, inconsistent income, three separate bank accounts she's trying to wrangle into some kind of order—decided her Needs envelope covers rent ($1200), utilities ($200), groceries ($300), and gas ($100). That's $1800 a month, or $450 a week.

One week she checks in and sees she's thirty dollars over in groceries. She didn't plan it. A friend invited her to a last-minute dinner and she said yes and picked up the tab. Now she's looking at $420 left in Needs with five days until her next paycheck.

Old Sarah would have spiraled. She'd have felt guilty, maybe skipped the check-in entirely next week out of shame, maybe abandoned the whole budget and gone back to winging it.

New Sarah—the one using this system—just shrugs and makes a note: pack lunch Monday through Wednesday, skip the fancy coffee on Thursday, problem solved. Or, if it's been a good month, she pulls thirty bucks from Savings to cover it and moves on. No drama. No guilt. Just a small course correction.

That's the entire point. You're not trying to be perfect. You're trying to *stay in the game*. And the only way to stay in the game is to make the game easy enough that you don't quit.

The weekly check-in also gives you a place to catch stuff *before* it becomes a crisis. Maybe you notice your utility bill was higher than usual this month—turns out the AC's been running nonstop because the thermostat's broken. You catch it now instead of three months from now when you're wondering why you're always short on cash. Or maybe you see you've been consistently *under*spending in one category—your Wants envelope has two hundred bucks sitting unused because you've been too busy to do much beyond work and sleep. That's useful information too. Maybe you reallocate that money. Maybe you give yourself permission to actually use it. Either way, you're making an active choice instead of just letting money sit there unnoticed.

One more thing about the weekly check-in: do it the same day every week. Sunday night works for a lot of people. Friday afternoon works for others. Pick a time, set a recurring reminder on your phone, and stick to it. The consistency matters more than the specific day. You're building a habit, and habits need rhythm.

Alright. Automation's running. Weekly check-ins are handling the small stuff. Now let's zoom out.

Every three months, you do a bigger review. Not a teardown. Not a rebuild. A *tune-up*. You're looking at patterns, not transactions. You're asking: is this system still serving me, or has my life changed in a way that means I need to adjust?

Pull up the last three months of spending. You don't need a spreadsheet for this—most banking apps will show you trends by category. Look for surprises. Look for drift. Look for categories where you're consistently over or under what you budgeted.

Let's say you initially put a hundred dollars a month into "Entertainment" but you've barely used fifty of it for three months straight. That's a signal. Maybe you've been busier than usual. Maybe your priorities have shifted. Maybe you'd rather put that extra fifty toward a vacation fund or your emergency savings. Whatever the reason, the money should go where it's *actually* useful, not sit in a category you allocated six months ago and never revisited.

Or flip it: maybe you budgeted two hundred a month for groceries and you're consistently hitting two-fifty. That's also a signal. Maybe grocery prices have gone up. Maybe you're cooking at home more and eating out less, which is great, but it means your food budget needs to expand and your restaurant budget can shrink. Adjust accordingly.

The quarterly review is also when you check in on your bigger goals. Are you on track to build that emergency fund? Are you saving enough for the down payment, the vacation, the new laptop, whatever target you set back in Chapter 5? If yes—celebrate. Seriously. Acknowledge the progress. If no—figure out why. Maybe you need to cut back somewhere else. Maybe your goal timeline was too aggressive and needs to stretch out a bit. Maybe something unexpected came up and derailed things, and that's okay, but now you need a plan to get back on track.

Let's go back to Sarah. After three months of using the system, she's noticing a pattern: her transportation costs are way higher than she thought. She budgeted a hundred bucks a month, figuring that would cover gas and the occasional rideshare. But she's been averaging closer to a hundred and sixty because she's been taking Lyft to client meetings more often than she expected.

So she's got options. She could increase the transportation line in her Needs envelope and pull that extra sixty from somewhere else—maybe Wants, maybe she cancels a subscription she's not using. Or she could look for ways to reduce the cost—take the bus more often, batch client meetings so she's not making as many trips, ask clients if they're open to Zoom calls instead of in-person. Either way, she's making a *conscious* decision instead of just watching her budget slowly bleed out without knowing why.

She also notices she's been consistently underspending in her Wants envelope. She thought she'd spend a hundred and fifty a month on clothes, books, random stuff. But it turns out she's only using about eighty. That extra seventy bucks a month? She reallocates it to a travel fund. Now, instead of that money just sitting there unused, it's actively working toward something she actually wants—a weekend getaway later in the year.

That's what the quarterly review gives you: the chance to make your budget fit your *actual* life instead of the life you thought you'd be living when you first set the thing up.

Here's a simple checklist you can use:

1. Review spending patterns in each envelope. 2. Check progress toward savings goals. 3. Identify any new or changing expenses. 4. Adjust allocations as needed. 5. Celebrate wins—even small ones.

Write that down. Stick it somewhere you'll see it. And every three months, work through it. Shouldn't take more than an hour. Less, once you've done it a few times and know what you're looking for.

Now let's make this even more concrete. I want you to picture a weekly rhythm—a fifteen-minute routine that keeps the whole system humming along without eating your life. I call it the Weekly Reset, and it has four steps:

Step 1: Automated Transfer Check. Just verify that your transfers are still happening. Banks occasionally glitch. Apps update and reset settings. Accounts get flagged for weird security reasons. Takes thirty seconds to confirm the money's moving where it's supposed to. If something's off, fix it before it snowballs.

Step 2: Envelope Balance Review. Look at each envelope. Where are you at? Anything significantly off from where you expected to be? If yes, note it. If no, great, move on.

Step 3: Next Week's Planning. Scan your calendar. Do you have anything coming up that might hit your budget? A birthday dinner you need to bring a gift to. A work trip where you'll need to front some costs and get reimbursed later. A doctor's appointment with a copay. Just flag it mentally so you're not blindsided.

Step 4: Gratitude and Adjustment. This one's going to sound touchy-feely, but bear with me. Take ten seconds and acknowledge one thing you did well this week with money. Maybe you didn't impulse-buy something. Maybe you packed lunch instead of eating out. Maybe you just *stuck with the system* even though it would have been easier to ignore it. Notice that. And then pick *one* thing you're going to adjust or improve next week. One. Not five. One.

That's the Weekly Reset. Automation check, balance review, quick planning scan, gratitude and adjustment. Fifteen minutes, tops. And it keeps you from ever getting so far off track that you need a massive overhaul to recover.

I know some of you are reading this and thinking it sounds easy. Maybe too easy. Like, "If it's this simple, why doesn't everyone do it?"

Because simple doesn't mean effortless. And because most people are trying to run a system that demands too much from them, and when they can't sustain it, they blame themselves instead of the system.

Here's what I've learned after years of watching people try to budget: the ones who succeed aren't the ones with the most discipline. They're the ones who build a system that *doesn't require* much discipline. They automate what they can. They check in regularly but briefly. They adjust when things change. They don't try to be perfect. They just try to stay aware.

You might be wondering: what about the 'spending rulebook' idea from earlier? How does that fit into all this?

Good question. (See, I told you I'd pause to address objections.)

The rulebook isn't a separate thing—it's just a way to make your weekly check-ins and quarterly reviews easier. When you sit down to look at your envelopes, you're not trying to remember what each category is *for*. You've already written it down.

For example: your Fun envelope gets a hundred and fifty dollars a month. Your rule might be, "Fun is for spontaneous stuff—concerts, movies, that weird little vintage shop downtown. It is *not* for online shopping when I'm bored at midnight." That's specific. That's useful. When you're tempted to buy something online at midnight, you don't have to debate with yourself in the moment—you just check the rule. If it doesn't fit, you don't buy it. Simple.

Or let's say your Needs envelope includes groceries. Your rule: "Groceries only. No gas-station snacks, no impulse candy at checkout, no fancy cheese I don't actually need just because it's on sale." Again—specific. Harder to rationalize your way around.

You don't need a hundred rules. Just a few clear guidelines for the categories where you know you tend to drift. Write them down in your notebook or type them into a note on your phone. Reference them during your weekly check-in. Adjust them during your quarterly review if they're not working.

The rulebook gives you clarity. And clarity is the thing that lets you make decisions quickly, without guilt, without second-guessing. "Does this fit the rule?" If yes, spend. If no, don't. Done.

Let me show you how all this works in practice with someone who's not Sarah. Let's call him David. He's a middle-school teacher, makes about five grand a month after taxes, and he's been trying to budget for *years* but keeps falling back into chaos because every system he's tried has been too complicated to maintain.

David decides: Needs get $2500. Wants get $750. Savings get $1000. Fun gets $750.

His rulebook looks like this:

Needs ($2500): Rent, utilities, car stuff, groceries. Sub-rule: eating out is limited to twice a month, budgeted here, not in Fun.

Wants ($750): Clothes, hobbies, the couple of streaming services he actually uses. Rule: before buying any clothing over a hundred bucks, wait twenty-four hours. If he still wants it the next day *and* it fits the budget, he can get it.

Savings ($1000): Split sixty-forty between an emergency fund and a vacation fund. Rule: automatic transfers on the fifth of every month—six hundred to emergency, four hundred to vacation.

Fun ($750): Concerts, going out with friends, spontaneous stuff. Rule: no impulse purchases over fifty bucks without checking the balance first. If the envelope's empty, wait until next month.

During his first quarterly review, David realizes he's been ordering takeout way more than he thought—like a hundred and fifty bucks a month. That wasn't even on his radar when he set up the system. So he adds a rule: limit takeout to once a week, budget sixty bucks a month for it in Needs, and take the other ninety and put it toward paying down his car loan faster.

He also has a big goal: he wants to save twenty thousand dollars for a down payment on a house over the next five years. That's four grand a year, or roughly three hundred and thirty-three dollars a month. He sets up an automatic transfer from his Savings envelope into a separate "House Fund" account. Every month, on the fifth, three thirty-three moves over. He doesn't see it. He doesn't think about it. It just accumulates.

And here's the thing: once David has these rules in place, he doesn't need to agonize over every purchase. He's not sitting there at 10:47 pm on a Sunday wondering if he's a good person or a bad person because he spent twelve dollars on a burrito. He just asks: does this fit my rulebook? If yes, great. If no, he skips it or adjusts something else to make room.

The system takes the *emotion* out of it. That's the whole point.

You might be thinking: what about emergencies? What about when life throws something at you that doesn't fit neatly into Needs or Wants or Fun?

That's what the Emergency Fund inside your Savings envelope is for. Car breaks down. Surprise medical bill. Fridge dies and you need a new one. The fund absorbs the hit. You don't have to scramble. You don't have to blow up your budget. You just pull from the fund, and then over the next few months, you rebuild it.

And if the emergency is bigger than the fund can handle? You adjust. You pull from other categories temporarily. You figure it out. The system doesn't solve every problem—it just gives you a framework to respond without panicking.

One last thing before we wrap this up. You set a reminder on your phone earlier—six months from now, to do a Budget Reset. That's when you go through the full checklist: review your core categories, pull three months of statements and look for spending leaks, check in on your savings goals, update your fixed expenses, future-proof for upcoming irregular costs, revisit your Fun budget, recalculate your allocations if needed, and document the changes.

It's the same idea as the quarterly review, just a little deeper. And it ensures that even if life changes—job changes, relationship changes, kids, moves, whatever—your budget changes *with* you instead of becoming this rigid thing you're trying to force yourself to fit into.

Don't be afraid to adjust. Don't be afraid to admit something isn't working. The only failure here is refusing to adapt.

So here's where we are. You've got automation running in the background, moving money where it needs to go without you lifting a finger. You've got a weekly fifteen-minute check-in to make sure you're still on track. You've got a quarterly or six-month review to zoom out and adjust for bigger shifts. And you've got a rulebook that gives you clarity when you're tempted to spend on something that doesn't fit.

That's the system. That's the whole thing.

No spreadsheets. No hours of data entry. No guilt spirals when you mess up. Just a rhythm that keeps you aware, keeps you aligned with your priorities, and doesn't ask more of your attention than you have to give.

Now—grab your notebook. Right now, before you turn the page. Write down three things:

1. Your current Needs, Wants, Savings, and Fun allocations. 2. One spending leak you're going to tackle this week. Just one. 3. One small savings goal you want to hit in the next six months.

That's it. Don't overthink it. Don't make it complicated. Just write it down.

Because here's what happens next—and this is the part nobody tells you when they hand you a budget template: the system only works if you *use* it. Not perfectly. Not flawlessly. Just consistently. And the only way to build consistency is to start. Today. Right now. With something small and concrete.

You've spent chapters learning the why and the how. You know the framework. You've seen the examples. You've got the tools.

Now the question is: what's the first move?

Also in the Series

Every book in Money Reset stands on its own — read them in any order. If this one was useful, the library continues:

Tax Strategies to Keep What You Earn

Salary Negotiation Before You Sign

Budgeting for People Who Hate Budgeting

Budgeting From Zero

Budgeting on an Irregular Income

Couples Budgeting

Budgeting After Debt

Budgeting for the Broke Paycheck

Budgeting for Impulse Spending

Budgeting for a Bigger Life

www.ingramcontent.com/pod-product-compliance
Lightning Source LLC
LaVergne TN
LVHW010725061126
851857LV00014B/1341
* 9 7 8 1 8 0 4 2 8 2 6 3 2 *